THIS BOOK
BELONGS TO

VINTAGE WEDDING STYLE

VINTAGE WEDDING STYLE

MORE THAN 25 SIMPLE PROJECTS AND
ENDLESS INSPIRATION FOR DESIGNING YOUR BIG DAY

Elizabeth Demos

CHRONICLE BOOKS

SAN FRANCISCO

Page 201 constitutes a continuation of the copyright page.

Library of Congress Cataloging-in-Publication Data:
Demos, Elizabeth.
 Vintage wedding style : more than 25 simple projects and endless inspiration for designing your big day / Elizabeth Demos.
    p. cm.
 Includes bibliographical references and index.
 ISBN 978-1-4521-0209-2
1. Weddings—Planning. 2. Wedding decorations. I. Title.

 HQ745.D46 2012
 392.5—dc23
                              2011042835

Manufactured in China

Designed by Kristen Hewitt
Additional editing by Janice Shay

Airstream is a registered trademark of Airstream, Inc. Dremel is a registered
trademark of Robert Bosch Tool Corporation. eBay is a registered trademark
of eBay Inc. Facebook is a registered trademark of Facebook, Inc. Hermès Paris
is a registered trademark of Hermès International. Rice Krispies is a registered
trademark of Kellogg Company Corp. X-ACTO is a registered trademark of Elmer's
Products, Inc. Zuber is a registered trademark of Manufacture de Papiers Peints
Zuber et Cie Corp.

10 9 8 7 6 5 4 3 2

Chronicle Books LLC
680 Second Street
San Francisco, California 94107
www.chroniclebooks.com

Contents

Introduction

Something old, something new . . .

THE BEST WEDDINGS TELL STORIES—stories of a bride and a groom, family, friends, and the heirlooms and memories of generations before them. When I first meet with clients, the initial conversation is often filled with dreams of how they imagine their wedding day. I take a lot of notes, ask and answer many questions, and look at scores of photos, all the while obtaining insight into their story—their family history, special traditions they want to include, and their taste. I share my love of vintage with all of my couples and help them incorporate vintage elements into their event.

Wedding inspiration is everywhere, but for me it is firmly rooted in the past. I'm a big believer in incorporating vintage treasures into our lives in new and modern ways. I adore the layered quality—the magical feeling of old meets new—that antique and vintage pieces bring to an event. I'm an old-fashioned girl in a modern world, and refreshing traditions is my expertise. Vintage wedding style, as I define it, is not the exact replication of a specific era. Instead, it incorporates some details from an era or a time and refreshes and updates them to make a wedding truly unique. The couples featured in this book appreciated historical references, antiques, and vintage goods—and each achieved a vintage style that was just right for them.

You'll see a Gatsby revival wedding that was inspired by the feeling of a leisurely afternoon in celebration; a circus-themed wedding that captures youthful and colorful memories of the circus; and an Airstream elopement that proves you can include style into even the smallest affair. Each wedding story offers inspiring photos, styling ideas, helpful tips, and DIY projects so you can replicate some of the details on your own. You will find creative ideas for everything from save-the-date cards to cake stands to party favors. I explain how to edit your ideas (a very important step!) and how to navigate common problems such as out-of-the-way locations, weather concerns, and budget. I also include a range of color palettes, inventive uses for old objects, and creative ways to help you discover your own personal wedding style. At the back, I share my favorite shops and resources where you can find the items and materials used in these weddings. I hope you feel motivated to check out the nearest flea market, estate sale, or antique shop to hunt for pieces that will make your event unique and memorable.

My favorite weddings are those that are true expressions of the couple, tell a story, and seamlessly marry the past and present. How do you envision your wedding day?

MUTUAL FRIEND.

REVIVING GATSBY

REVIVING GATSBY

RELAXING, INTIMATE, HISTORIC—sometimes the idea for a wedding starts with how you want it to feel, rather than how it will look. For this wedding, the couple had very strong ideas about the mood they wanted to establish. They wanted their friends to be relaxed and enjoy the day, and they wanted the feel of a private mansion wedding. They imagined an outdoor venue that was both gracious and intimate, but casual enough that everyone could have fun. I understood the couple's vision for a day of celebration grounded in a much earlier—and simpler—way of life.

Their needs brought to mind F. Scott Fitzgerald's descriptions of lawn parties at historic old mansions by the sea—slow, easy days filled with champagne and band music. Everything about this wedding at Sapelo Island off the Georgia coast had the feel of an updated scene from *The Great Gatsby*. The atmosphere of that era was what I wanted to help them achieve.

The venue, Sapelo Island, can only be reached by ferry, which runs on a limited schedule. That ensured privacy for the day's events. The island boasts one inn—a lovely old plantation home, the Reynolds Mansion. The many descendants of the island's first inhabitants populate the island and maintain its historic feel. The leaves of beautiful, ancient oaks rustle in the breeze off the ocean, and the well-appointed grounds of the home draw guests outdoors to talk, read, and relax.

If you worry about other guests at a hotel intruding on your wedding party, privacy may be as important to you as it was for this couple. Think about finding an estate, a farm, or a private home where you can be assured that your day—or weekend—is for you and your guests, and no one else. Of course, privacy comes at a price and requires certain considerations. We were unable to find a florist who would deliver to the island. Vendors would only deliver to the ferry departure dock on the mainland. So we had to bring all the flowers—and everything else that would normally be delivered—and arrange them on-site. I don't suggest doing your own wedding flowers, unless you have someone you really trust to style the floral arrangements the day before or the day of the wedding. Making your own bouquet, corsages, and boutonnieres is time-consuming, and you will want to focus on other things.

When you take on a project yourself, enlist an army of family members and friends to help, as we did. We put people to work carrying truckloads of flowers, boxes, and other items. Planning an event for a remote locale such as this requires that you be super organized and keep lists of everything you need to bring in. For shipping or transporting materials to your site, you want to use, if possible, nonbreakable items and choose lightweight decorations—you'll save a bundle on shipping costs. Before you load up on a lot of breakable things, see what your location can offer. If something is broken in transit, you may not be able to get a replacement.

Once we established the mood for the celebration and selected a venue to exude that feeling, we created a visual theme for the day that reflected the Gatsby era. This is where you can get creative and explore what materials, colors, foods, drinks, and music can convey the mood you're going for. This couple chose cleverly worded stationery that incorporated vintage-style typefaces—invitations are always a great way to further the aesthetic of your event and give your guests a hint of what's to come. For this wedding, when the guests boarded the ferry for the twenty-minute journey, they were presented with a Western Union telegram with information about Sapelo Island, along with a package of replica postcards. The postcards were printed with a schedule for the weekend, a map, and the history of both the island and the Reynolds Mansion.

Throughout the course of the wedding, you want to have items that relate to the theme of the day. With a little planning, you can carry your inspiration from the invitation to the favors, colors, and accoutrements of the event. It is your mood board realized. Thankfully, my habit of hoarding vintage props came in handy. For this wedding, I brought along boxes of treasures, some from my collection, others created for the occasion—doll chairs to display the wedding rings; a handmade ring pillow with vintage

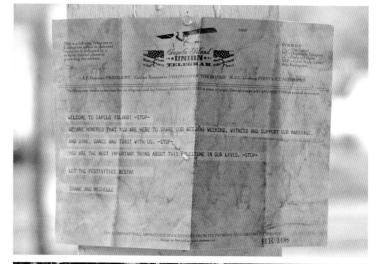

TIP

Some couples have refined a color palette before they visit their wedding or reception venue. Consider, instead, taking color cues for your wedding from your chosen location. For this wedding, a quick glance suggested a palette of teal, off-white, brown, and hints of gold to replace the silver colors the bride had originally thought would work. Keep your eyes open, and you might find that the perfect palette already exists within your wedding location.

A GRAND EXHIBITION OF LOVE AND ADVENTURE!

Together with their parents

MICHELLE LEE
THE MISTRESS OF EBULLIENT ELOCUTION & ELECTRO-MAGNETISM

and

SHANE JOINER
JOCULAR JACK-OF-ALL-TRADES & MASTER OF MYSTERY

INVITE YOU ON A VOYAGE TO THE GEORGIA COAST TO WITNESS THEIR

WEDDING

Saturday, the Thirtieth of October
Two Thousand and Ten
AT ELEVEN-THIRTY (ANTE MERIDIEM)
FOLLOWED BY GEECHEE FARE & ISLAND TOURS
at R.J. Reynolds Mansion
ON THE SERENE ISLE OF SAPELO
✦ TAKE NOTICE! ✦

RSVP HERE: WWW.SHANEANDMICH.COM

"MORE ENTERTAINMENT THAN YOU CAN SHAKE A SNAKE AT"

CEREMONY AND RECEPTION

11:30am - Wedding ceremony

12pm - Hors d'oeuvres
and celebratory drink during
family pictures, band begins

12:30pm - First dance.
Father of the Bride toast,
followed by Geechee fare
and desserts

2:30 and 3:15pm (optional)-
Island Tour, History and
Sights of Sapelo (beach,
Hog Hammock, Lighthouse)

3pm (optional) -
GA/FL game in Game Room

4:00pm - Bon voyage

GEORGIA'S LAND of the GOLDEN ISLES

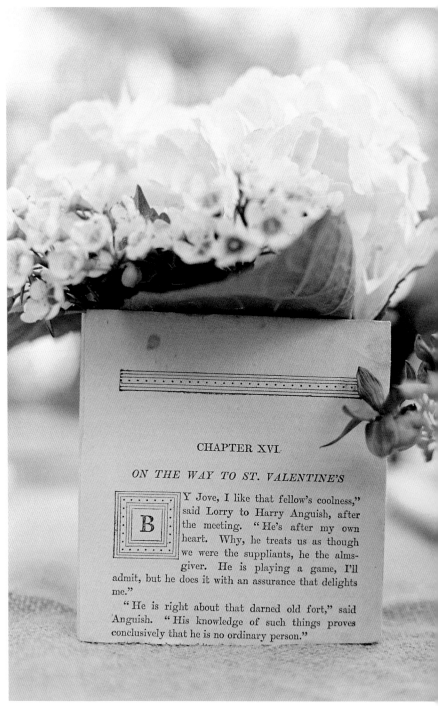

ribbon ties; playing cards printed with the emblem used on the wedding invitations; and pillows screen-printed with the couple's initials. Each element reflected the vintage look. If you're not a hoarder, think about other resources you have at your disposal— a grandparent's attic, eBay, estate sales, or flea markets may provide the accessories you need.

Sometimes small elements are the most effective way to create a vintage feeling. In this case, the elements were the paper boxes used as containers for the flower arrangements—remember, we didn't want to transport glass vases to the island! I covered the affordable, generic boxes with pages from old books. The yellowed pages beautifully complemented the couple's theme.

Although I didn't plan it, many of the pages were from love stories, the perfect choice for this particular love story. The flower girl's basket, also made of vintage papers, lent continuity to the vintage feel of the ceremony.

After the wedding, we spread old quilts on the lawn and scattered custom-made screen-printed monogrammed pillows around. People listened to music, danced, talked, and played cards while they sipped champagne, chatted with the newly-weds, and enjoyed themselves and the island, as if they owned it for the day.

TIP

Destination weddings can be a lot of fun for your guests. This couple welcomed guests with a cocktail party and a ghost tour of the mansion, held a late-night costume party (they were married on a Halloween weekend), and hosted a brunch the day after the wedding. You don't have to fill every day with activities—you could simply compile a list of interesting local places to visit, sites to see, and places to eat. You could even negotiate special group prices for venues that require tickets.

Hard to believe, but there are quite a few tucked away wedding destinations with little or no presence on the Internet. If you want to learn more about your destination or venue, a Google image search might turn up helpful photos of other weddings that have occurred there. Also check on the photographer's site, since photographers tend to capture special details of a location that the venue's management might fail to mention. You could even reach out to other couples who have been married there. This bride and groom found a couple that freely shared all they learned after having their wedding on the island.

PAPER-COVERED BOX CENTERPIECES

If you need light, portable props for your wedding, you want to make them from paper or soft goods. You can slip store-bought plastic cups into these paper-covered boxes. No one will ever know or see what holds the water—just that the flower containers look beautiful. The gift boxes come with lids. You can cover these as well and use them as pedestals for bud vases.

HOW TO

1. **Set up your work area.** Choose a work surface in a well-ventilated area, and cover the surface with butcher paper. Remove the lids from the boxes and set them aside, then line up the boxes according to size.

2. **Cut up the book.** Using the craft knife, cut all the pages from the book. Take advantage of any interesting illustrations or text that might fit your wedding style. Separate the pages if they are stuck together.

3. **Cover the boxes.** Wearing rubber gloves, apply a light, even coat of spray adhesive to one side of a page. Allow the adhesive to set up for a few seconds. Align the left edge of the page against the edge of one side of a box. Wrap the page around to the second side of the box. Apply adhesive to another page, and let the adhesive set up. Position the page on the second side of the box so that it overlaps the first page, and then wrap around to the third side of the box. Add pages to the third and fourth sides in the same way. The fourth page will wrap around to the first side of the box. Use the craft knife to trim the paper flush with the top and bottom edges of the box. Repeat until each box is covered. Set the boxes aside until they are completely dry.

4. **Cover the lids.** Use the ruler to measure the height of the side of a lid. Cut a page so that it is larger than the lid on all sides by that measurement. Center the top of the lid on the paper. Choose one corner to cover first. Use the scissors to make a cut from the edge of the paper straight in to meet that corner. The cut creates two tabs—one that will fold flush with the side of the box and one that will overhang. Fold and crease the tab that is flush. Then, wrap the longer tab around the corner of the box and fold and crease. Repeat the cutting and creasing for the remaining corners. Smooth out the page and apply a light, even coat of spray adhesive. Allow the adhesive to set up for a few seconds. Place the top of the lid on the sprayed side of the page, and neatly fold up the page to cover the sides. Repeat until each lid is covered. Set the lids aside until they are completely dry, and you are ready to set up your venue.

LEVEL:
Easy

WHEN TO START:
3 weeks before the wedding

YIELD:
50 flags

MATERIALS
• 6 yd/5.5 m ribbon in varying
  widths and colors
• Fifty 10-in/25-cm wooden skewers

TOOLS
• Ruler
• Scissors
• Hot glue gun
• Hot glue sticks

PETITE RIBBON FLAGS

Adding tiny ribbon flags to individual flower arrangements gives your table settings a festive and cohesive look. They also add a decorative touch to your wedding cake or desserts. You can cut the skewers to vary the heights using a craft knife.

HOW TO

1. **Cut the ribbon.** Using the ruler and scissors, cut the ribbon into fifty 3- to 4-in/7.5- to 10-cm lengths.

2. **Glue the ribbon.** Run a bead of hot glue as long as the ribbon is wide down the top of a skewer. Press the glued skewer onto one end of a length of ribbon. Allow the glue to set for a few seconds. Wrap the ribbon around the skewer to conceal it. Run a bead of glue where the ribbon overlaps; this will secure the flag and prevent the ribbon from uncurling and exposing the wood. Keep pressure on the ribbon until the glue has cooled, about 10 seconds. Repeat to make the remaining flags.

3. **Finish the flags.** Perfect the look of each flag by cutting a forked tongue into the tail of every ribbon.

ORNATE DRESS HANGER

A quintessential image in modern wedding photo albums is the still life with dress. Having the right hanger on hand to showcase your beautiful wedding gown is a must. Skip the usual padded variety and customize your own. It will make a nice keepsake. If your hanger spins around, consider finishing the back with a few leaves to disguise the underside of your embellishments. For an aged look, you can lightly sand the edges of your painted hanger to reveal some of the wood surface.

HOW TO

1. **Prepare your work surface.** Cover a table with butcher paper. Fill the bowl with paint.

2. **Paint the hanger.** Wearing rubber gloves and using the paintbrush, paint the wooden surface of the hanger. Let it dry for about 5 minutes. Add a second coat if needed.

3. **Create the decoration.** Layer the leaves, flowers, buttons, and ribbon into an eye-catching arrangement. Rely on the leaves to form the base, then cluster the next pieces on top, finishing with the smallest elements. When you are done, work backward and remove each layer, placing it on the work surface.

4. **Attach the decoration to the hanger.** Apply a dab of hot glue to the center of the hanger, just below the hook. Press the leaves into the glue, and let them set for a second or two. Add the next layers, attaching each with very small amounts of hot glue. Finish the hanger with a hanging ribbon or two, and use the scissors to trim the ends.

LEVEL:
Easy

WHEN TO START:
1 week before the wedding

YIELD:
1 hanger

MATERIALS
- Acrylic paint in selected color
- Wooden hanger (vintage or new)
- Assorted embellishments including millinery flowers, leaves, old buttons, and ribbon

TOOLS
- Butcher paper
- Small bowl
- Rubber gloves
- Small paintbrush
- Hot glue gun
- Hot glue stick
- Scissors

STYLING IDEA

Pillows, quilts, and throws can enhance and personalize the furnishings at your wedding location. Soft goods are a nice way to perk up rental furniture, too. You can customize store-bought pillows with an icon from your invitations, your new monogram, or words that are meaningful to you. Local monogram stores and screen-printing studios are terrific resources for this sort of detail. Throws come in handy for guests if your wedding or reception will be outdoors in a cool climate.

TWO-RING CIRCUS

TICKET

Chapter
No. 2

TWO-RING CIRCUS

WHEN MY GOOD FRIEND Halli first approached me about her wedding, I knew it would be a fun-filled event. She and Adam had a vision, but limited time and long distance from the location of their wedding made the planning hard. They wanted bright colors, vintage elements, and a casual, playful atmosphere. Halli shared her save-the-date, some color cues, and loads of images to help me visualize what she had in mind. Sometimes a single color or other element will open the floodgates of inspiration. In this case, the image on their save-the-date expressed their fondness for small circuses and county fairs.

I created a storyboard that included all the bride's must-haves and added many of my own. I filled the board with scraps of patterned fabric and paper, ribbon samples, crepe paper, balloons, millinery flowers, old-timey candy, vintage paper straws, carnival trinkets, and the like. All the while Halli had been doing the same—proof we were on the right track. A lot of those original elements found their way into the big day. That often happens, so go with your instinct because chances are your first ideas are the ones that are most true to who you and your fiancé are.

The menu gave a nod to the nostalgic fair atmosphere. After the ceremony, we fired up a popcorn maker, and a friend of the family contributed a cotton candy machine. You never know what amazing resources your friends will be—don't be shy about asking around for loaners before purchasing something you'll only use once. We served miniature hot dogs, sliders, and tiny corn on the cob in traditional red-and-white paper bowls. At a fry station on a separate table, we offered shoestring french fries in yellow-dotted paper cones. Among other treats were mac and cheese and coleslaw, presented in paper soufflé cups and eaten with wooden spoons and forks. The look was carried through to the beverages: red-and-white paper straws in classic Ball jar glasses for spiked punch, sweet tea, and water. Our favorite hometown bakery provided an old-fashioned tiered buttercream cake with a vintage-inspired topper.

To round out the celebration, we opened up the barn for dancing. It was strung inside and out with loads of café lights—one of the bride's must-haves. The barn's large overhang and central closed area lent themselves beautifully to a natural flow from dining and socializing outside to dancing indoors. All the food was served outside in a covered area. The only dilemma was getting people to move from one area to the other. The inspiration for my solution came from the big-top theme. I asked one of the bride's friends to periodically carry signs through the crowd that read "First Dance" and "Cake Cutting," while ringing a little hand bell. Find the master coordinators among your friends, pick someone who's outgoing, and appoint that person to be your ringmaster, helping to move your guests seamlessly from one event or location to the next. The strategy works like a charm and is especially helpful if your location has a strict end time for the festivities.

If you're going for a playful atmosphere or will include many children, come up with games and activities for both young and old. We settled on a picture booth where guests placed their faces in a cutout, and a separate kissing booth. For the latter, guests received tickets with their wedding invitations that read "Good for one kiss from the bride or groom." The groom's father, a gifted furniture maker, constructed both booths, and a terrific sign maker created the graphics. For kids, you could do what we did: roll brown craft paper on a long harvest table and set out jars of crayons. This will occupy them for hours.

To add a bit of color and festivity, we hung lengths of yellow-and-white-striped fabric from the rafters of the barn to suggest the feeling of being inside a circus tent. We filled the space with extra-large balloons and red-and-white tissue-paper pinwheels to enhance the circus theme. This barn happened to be very attractive, but if you need to mask any unsightly features at your venue, swagging fabric and hanging a few large objects are good solutions.

From the vintage truck that brought the bride to the wedding to the old-timey straw fans provided for everyone, no detail was overlooked. Incorporating all the different elements this very special couple wanted was a true balancing act. I felt like the "ringleader" but, thankfully, did not have to jump through rings of fire.

TIP *Concession suppliers and restaurant equipment companies are excellent resources for specialty food packaging like the cute plaid bowls and dotted paper cones used in this wedding. Concession suppliers are also a good source for vintage-looking candy and popcorn and cotton candy machines.*

FREE KISS

GOOD FOR ONE
FREE KISS
TO BE REDEEMED AT THE KISSING BOOTH
GOOD ONLY SATURDAY MAY 9, 2009
Offer is limited to one kiss per person.

MARTHA B. NORRIS & THE LATE R. AUBREY NORRIS
INVITE YOU TO CELEBRATE THE MARRIAGE OF

KARI HALLIGAN NORRIS
&
ADAM BRADFORD SMITH

SATURDAY, MAY 9TH, 2009
AT 5:00

Meldrim Plantation
10673 Meldri Road
Brooklet, GA

(Dinner and Dancing to Follow)

TIP *Don't just relegate a vintage car or truck to the getaway. Consider using your transportation to deliver you to the ceremony or use the vehicle in your photos. Vintage car collectors and clubs can be found in every community. They might not let you drive the car, but they often include their chauffeur services in their fee.*

RED-AND-WHITE PINWHEELS

Paper projects are an inexpensive and effective way to inject color and whimsy into your wedding decor. These pinwheels are constructed with paper buntings. The traditional bunting is made of consecutively hung pleated half circles. When opened up, they look like fans and can be hung as a garland. Decorations like these can be customized to express the theme of your wedding.

HOW TO

1. **Unfold the buntings.** If your buntings are joined into a garland, cut them apart with scissors. Open each bunting into a half circle.

2. **Create the pinwheels.** The long edge of each pleated paper half circle is attached to a strip of cardboard. Working with two half circles, sparingly apply beads of hot glue to the cardboard of one half circle. Carefully press the cardboard of the second half circle onto the first, aligning the cardboard strips. Let the glue set for 10 seconds. Repeat to make the second pinwheel.

3. **Hang the pinwheels.** Punch a hole in each pinwheel near one end of the glued cardboard. Thread baker's twine through the hole. Cut the twine, knot it into a loop, and hang the pinwheels.

LEVEL:
Easy

WHEN TO START:
3 weeks before the wedding

YIELD:
50 napkin rings

MATERIALS
· Scraps of vintage cotton fabric,
  ribbon, or burlap
· 50 fabric table napkins

TOOLS
· Ruler
· Scissors
· Hot glue gun
· Hot glue sticks

VINTAGE FABRIC NAPKIN RINGS

Even small scraps of fabric are handy for making napkin rings. For fun and variety, you can choose an assortment of fabrics in multiple colors and textures that reflect the palette of your wedding. You can use scraps from items created for your wedding such as tablecloths, bridesmaid dresses, or the ring bearer's pillow.

HOW TO

1. **Cut the fabric strips.** Using the ruler and scissors, cut the fabric into fifty strips, each 1.5 in/4 cm wide and 5 in/12 cm long. Leave the edges raw.

2. **Glue the rings.** Roll each napkin and wrap it with a fabric strip. Hold the strip so that the edges overlap slightly. Apply a dab of hot glue to the end of the bottom strip. Press both ends together for a few seconds until the glue is set to finish.

TIP

Are you getting married in a place that won't allow the traditional rice toss? You can make little yarn pom-poms like the ones here and pass them out to guests as they arrive, along with instructions for when to toss them. As alternatives, you could use paper or flower blooms, confetti, or birdseed after the nuptials. Be sure to clear your choice with your venue to make sure it is approved.

STYLING IDEA

You can commission a sign painter or printing company to paint graphics on wooden panels for your event. Or, you can paint the signs yourself. They can announce the cake cutting, first dance, last dance, bouquet toss, garter toss, or send-off. Ask a friend to wander through the crowd carrying the signs, to alert guests when something momentous is about to happen. Think of having a sign for your exit that reads "just married" or "thank you." You and your groom can carry it as you make your getaway.

UP IN THE
CLOUDS

UP IN THE CLOUDS

THE ADVANTAGE OF DESTINATION WEDDINGS is that they are both a ceremony and a vacation—for you and your guests—and this idea can play significantly in your choice of a theme. The word *theme* may conjure up bad memories of prom dresses and bejeweled shoes, but themes can be tasteful, too, and make a ceremony memorable as well as fun. This beautiful travel-themed wedding is a great example—and there wasn't a prom dress or bejeweled shoe in sight.

Seth and Elizabeth were avid travelers, which influenced their chic coastal wedding—from the save-the-date incorporating a hand-drawn airplane to the sign-in table, the cake topper, and the candle favors wrapped in vintage maps. When you start to plan your wedding, think about the things that are meaningful to you and your fiancé—these items could be anything from books or bicycles to vintage board games or a specific place. Look around your home, through your photo albums, and at your collections. If you choose something that comes easily to you, I promise it will make your wedding planning a lot easier—and even more affordable because you'll be tapping into resources readily available to you.

The couple chose the Jekyll Island Club for their setting, the once exclusive vacation playground of tycoons and socialites like the Rockefellers, Morgans, Asters, Pulitzers, and Vanderbilts in the late 1800s and early 1900s. First and foremost, they selected the resort because of its proximity to the Georgia coast and the endless activities the island provides. The couple knew exactly what they wanted for the wedding—a quick ride to the beach on bicycles for the ceremony and a stop for ice cream on the return to the clubhouse. They wanted to keep the celebration casual, so the bride chose a locally designed, knee-length dress, and the groom wore a khaki suit with an airplane-print Hermès tie (a gift from the bride).

After the ceremony, guests were greeted on the croquet lawn of the club with Arnold Palmer cocktails. They were asked to sign their names on tiny paper flags. Drawing inspiration from the tacks you might place on a map after your travels, the couple had their guests pierce their flags with straight pins and mark their city of origin on a vintage map of the United States.

Sometimes a single object can inspire the entire look of a wedding. Much of the orange and aqua palette for this wedding was pulled from the map for the guests' sign-in table. The map, found at an antique fair, helped establish a strong color theme. It acted as my compass as I gathered other decorations and made other decisions. I scored a few extra maps and cut them up to make the covers for the favor candles. I had a stamp made from an image of an airplane and used it to stamp the gift bags. The muslin bags became instant packaging for the candles as guests left for the night. For inexpensive centerpieces, we grouped aqua-colored vintage bottles filled with soft white flowers on the tables. Doing clusters of small containers is a nice way to save on the cost of flowers, but still make a big color statement.

The wedding cake enhanced the travel idea. I found a little replica plane similar to the planes flown by the couple and perched it atop a three-tiered, blue fondant cake decorated with clouds. You can use your wedding cake creatively to express the theme of your wedding.

TIP *Incorporate your interests and those of your fiancé into the graphic scheme of your wedding. If you are film buffs, consider images from old films or come up with a play on words from your favorite film for your save-the-dates and invitations. Then use elements found in the movie's sets or a specific color palette from the film in your decor. Let's say you are foodies. Put an emphasis on the food selections and wine pairings. Word your invitation like a menu with the evening plotted out like courses.*

Save the Date

05.12.10

Elizabeth & Seth

TIP

It is never too early to set the tone for your event. Your save-the-dates and invitations are the first impression you make when you communicate with your guests. Choose colors and fonts that will be repeated on all your signage and paper goods such as programs, guest book, and favor tags.

LEVEL:
Easy

WHEN TO START:
3 weeks before the wedding

YIELD:
50 votive favors

MATERIALS
- One 8½-by-11-in/21.5-by-28-cm sheet card stock
- 50 straight-sided glass votive candle holders, each 2 in/5 cm wide by 2½ in/6 cm tall
- Vintage maps
- 50 unscented votive candles

TOOLS
- Pencil
- Scissors
- Clear tape
- Glue stick

VINTAGE MAP VOTIVE CANDLES

With a good theme in mind, you can scour local flea markets and antique shops for items that carry out your vision. Using maps was the perfect fit for this travel-happy couple. Vintage maps are colorful and filled with interesting lines. One large map will make approximately fifty favors, but if you find only smaller maps, you will want to purchase more than you need.

HOW TO

1. **Make a template.** Set the card stock on a flat surface. Lay a candle holder on its side on the card stock. Slowly roll it along the card stock, tracing the path of the holder with a pencil. To allow for an overlap, add ¼ in/6 mm to the length of the tracing. Cut out the template. Wrap it around the candle holder to check the size and fit.

2. **Cut out map pieces.** Place the template on a map, trace around the template with the pencil, and cut out the piece. Repeat to cut out the remaining pieces.

3. **Attach the map cutouts.** Secure one end of each cutout to a candle holder with a small piece of tape. Wrap the cutout around the holder and use the glue stick to glue the paper in place where the ends overlap and to conceal the tape. Insert a candle into each holder when ready to display.

MUSLIN FAVOR BAGS

You can dress up a simple favor with creative packaging. These little bags make for easy transport when guests are traveling. Plain muslin bags with drawstrings are often used for making tea, and are available at craft stores, specialty grocery stores, or retail supply stores online. You will want to purchase several more than you need, to allow for mistakes and to test the rubber stamp. Adorn the bags with an image that reflects your theme, and when your guests use them again, they will think of you and your one-of-a-kind wedding.

HOW TO

1. **Order your rubber stamp.** Custom rubber stamps can be ordered from a local or online source, in any size you like. Follow the stamp engraver's guidance for submitting your image. Because you will be applying fabric paint to the stamp, choose a clear, bold image without intricate details. Ask for a stamp with a simple wood handle. (Measure your muslin bag before you order your stamp, to ensure that the stamp's dimensions do not exceed the bag's surface.)

2. **Make a card stock liner.** Cut a piece of card stock that is at least as large as your stamp and will fit inside the muslin bags. The liner, slipped inside each bag before it is stamped, will prevent the fabric paint from bleeding through the front of the bag to the back.

3. **Prepare the paint and stamp.** Pour a small amount of fabric paint onto the paper plate. Roll the brayer into the paint, then roll it over the stamp. Apply a thin, but even layer of paint to the surface of the stamp. Use one of the muslin bags to determine the placement of the design and to practice making perfect images with the stamp.

4. **Stamp the bags.** Slide the card stock liner into a muslin bag and smooth out any wrinkles in the fabric. Use the brayer to coat the stamp with paint, then carefully place the stamp on the bag. Firmly press the stamp straight down and then lift it straight up. Remove the cardstock and lay the bag flat to dry. Insert the liner into another bag, cover the stamp with paint, and stamp the bag. Repeat to stamp the remaining bags.

Brides don't want to talk about the possibility of inclement weather, but the possibility is important to consider when your event will be held outdoors. You should have a back-up plan, be it a tent or nearby pavilion. Make sure you and your caterer are prepared to move your whole operation indoors or under cover.

Working with found objects to make an impromptu directional sign can be a lifesaver when your wedding is in a remote venue like the beach. Look around your location for inspiration. You can gather rocks, sticks, and flowers, then stack and line them up to form an arrow or spell words. Check first that your location doesn't have rules that restrict collecting natural materials.

STYLING IDEA

At an outdoor venue, fill a basket or other attractive container with paper parasols for the guests to shade themselves from the sun. They are inexpensive, come in a multitude of colors, and double as umbrellas in case it sprinkles during the ceremony or reception. By providing an alternative to the standard black umbrella, you can ensure that your photos will be bright and pretty regardless of the weather.

Fall Color

Chapter
No. 4

Fall Color

WHEN JESSICA AND I FIRST MET, we had an instant bond. The two of us were smiling ear to ear as we spent hours exchanging ideas and talking about the details for her wedding. I knew that this was a sure sign of great things to come. When you click with someone you're going to have a working relationship with, everything from brainstorming to decision making is just plain easier. Jessica told me about her love of soft autumn colors, her plan to be married outside in the fall, and her desire to include many handmade vintage-inspired details.

Jessica, an avid vintage clothing collector and dealer, happened upon the perfect dress and scooped it up, knowing she would wear it when she married her college sweetheart, Terry. Only one small detail stood between finding her perfect dress and the day she'd wear it: the proposal! Once Terry proposed, Jessica envisioned a sweet affair that reflected everything and everyone important to them. Because she comes from a family of crafters, seamstresses, and woodworkers, all of whom were happy to lend a hand when called upon, she was certain to have the wedding she wanted. If you aren't fortunate enough to have such a generous and gifted family, you can easily hire crafters and artisans to help execute your vision.

Jessica made a long list of items she wanted, and I did the same. Because of Jessica's experience, I was confident that her embroidered quilt squares, hand printed programs, and fabric flowers for adorning the bridesmaids' lanterns would be completed expertly and in time. She chose to have each attendant carry a lantern with a single candle inside. The lanterns with flowers on their handles were a substitute for the more traditional bouquet. This is a nice option if you don't want to splurge on flowers or you simply want something different.

I took my cue from Jessica when creating the centerpieces. I used vintage and new fabric flowers and combined them with some of her handmade flowers. The long tables were lined with runners cut from canvas drop cloths from the hardware store. On each runner sat an assortment of small tree stumps and jute-wrapped jars. Some of the jars held candles, while others had tall branches gathered from the woods. The branches created the height we needed without interfering with the sight lines, so that guests could carry on conversations with ease. Each branch was sparingly adorned with fabric flowers in taupe, mustard, and soft pink, to replicate forced flowering branches. The overall affect was both feminine and rustic, and therefore appealing to men and women alike.

Jessica brought the woodsy feeling into her treatment of linens. She crafted adornments using real and felted acorns, millinery leaves, and twine. Napkins were made with the same canvas as the runners, and were folded and tied with a cluster of the felted acorns. The same clusters were used to make boutonnieres for the groom and groomsmen.

TIP

Give your photographer a list of must-have images for your ceremony and reception. Don't overlook details that you want your photographer to record. If, for instance, your napkins match the groomsmen's bouton-nieres, note that you'd like close-up photos of both items. Present the list weeks before the wedding rather than the day before, so the photographer can bring the correct lenses and other equipment. Your photographer will thank you, and you will walk away knowing that all your memories have been recorded.

Finding ways to incorporate your groom in the planning process can be tricky. In Jessica and Terry's case, she handled most of the decorative details, and he contributed ideas for music, food, and photography. This dilemma is fairly common, but, rest assured, responsibilities and decisions can be shared evenly.

Jessica spent many hours assembling handmade flowers for her bridal bouquet. The vintage jewelry and buttons and the sparkly details she chose complemented her dress. She crafted her own garter, decorative pieces for her bridesmaids to wear in their hair, and even a collar for the couple's dog, Wicket, to wear as she went down the aisle. Once Jessica got going on making the flowers, there was no end in sight. She knew that I would find a place for them all.

The couple wanted their guests to mingle and dance, so they chose to serve a buffet dinner and to provide seating for every-one in a rustic pavilion. The menu included an assortment of organic delicacies from a local farm-to-table restaurant, a petite wedding cake for cutting, and cupcakes in various flavors from a much-loved corner bakery. Wanting the small cake to feel like a tiered cake, I decided to present it on two round layers created from a roll of jute webbing and a cake tin. The unique cake stand achieved the height we were after. A friend of the bride's embroidered the couple's initials on a piece of fabric and gave it to them shortly before the wedding. They decided to use it as a cake topper.

TIP

To avoid static wedding seating at tables, plan to offer gathering spots that encourage guests to move about and socialize. You can set up lounge areas near the bar; lawn games such as croquet, bocce ball, or corn hole; or a bonfire with nearby seating.

Throughout the night, guests waved small flags when they wanted to share a dance with the bride or groom. Jars holding the flags were placed on either side of a "tip" jar in which guests could drop spending money for the newlywed's honeymoon to Paris. Guests enjoyed this little tongue-in-cheek detail.

Depending on your location, an autumn wedding can be iffy, but thankfully the climate was temperate. We expected the temperature to drop as the sun went down, but rather than take the celebration indoors, we lit two small bonfires and surrounded them with pine benches. The bonfires added ambiance and encouraged gathering and conversation. We also provided ingredients and supplies to make s'mores. Self-serve stations like this are fun for guests of any age.

At the end of the evening, invitees were given screen-printed muslin bags that held buttons with illustrations drawn by the bride, and were encouraged to take a sampling of sweets and baked goods home. In exchange, guests were invited to write greetings on fabric quilt squares before they left. Later, Jessica embroidered each message and pieced the good wishes into a quilt. This lovely keepsake was the perfect memory of her "handmade" day.

TIP

If you are not a crafter, you can still incorporate handmade details. You can come up with the ideas, and the execution can be a group effort or can be hired out. Bridal attendants are always looking for ways to contribute, and a craft-themed bridal party is a great bonding opportunity. Supply the materials and instructions as well as a meal, and you have the formula for a fun and productive evening with friends.

FELTED ACORN BOUTONNIERES

You don't have to be a florist to create imaginative boutonnieres. They are the simplest of all the flower arrangements you can make for your event, and the groom will appreciate that you created them yourself. The handmade acorns and antique millinery leaves add a bit of vintage style, without being overly feminine. Because boutonnieres will be worn all day and will have to survive many hugs from well-wishers, these sturdy alternatives to real flowers are practical as well as attractive. They will also be a lasting memento.

HOW TO

1. **Make wool balls.** Wrap each piece of wool fiber around itself to create a dense ball about the size of a golf ball. Place the ball on the piece of foam. Stab the ball with the felting needle, being careful not to push the needle completely through the foam. Be mindful of your fingers, as the needle is very sharp. This process binds the fibers to one another and, as you work the wool, creates a denser and denser ball. From start to finish should be about 5 minutes, depending on how solid you want the balls to be.

2. **Attach the caps.** Apply a dab of hot glue to the inside of an acorn cap and press a wool ball into the cap. Let the glue set for 10 seconds. Repeat to make eleven more acorns.

3. **Assemble the boutonnieres.** Gather two acorns, two millinery leaves, four flower stamens, and one millinery flower. Trim the millinery leaf stems to 2 in/5 cm. Holding the two leaves, place each stamen in front of the leaves. Secure in place with a dab of hot glue and let set

for 10 seconds. Then glue each acorn in front of the leaves, again letting the glue set for 10 seconds. Fold the stamens in half, glue in place, and let the glue set for 10 seconds. Find a spot for the flower between the acorns and where it won't cover the stamens completely. Apply a dab of hot glue, adhere the flower, and let set for 10 seconds. Wrap all the stems with floral tape. Repeat to make five more boutonnieres.

4. **Attach the yarn.** Apply a dab of hot glue to the base of the leaves on the back of each boutonniere. Attach one end of yarn to the glue and let set for 10 seconds. Wrap the yarn down and around the stem, completely covering the floral tape. Cut the yarn and secure the end to the bottom of the boutonniere with a dab of hot glue, again letting the glue set for 10 seconds.

5. **Finish the boutonnieres.** Push a boutonniere pin into the back of each stem.

LEVEL:
Moderate

WHEN TO START:
4 weeks before the wedding

YIELD:
6 boutonnieres

MATERIALS

- 12 pieces of wool fiber, also known as wool roving, about 6 by 8 in/ 15 by 20 cm
- 12 acorn caps (gathered yourself or purchased online)
- 12 millinery leaves with wire spines
- 24 stems of artificial flower stamens
- 6 small millinery flowers
- Green floral tape
- 1 yd/1 m yarn
- 6 boutonniere pins

TOOLS

- 5 by 5 by 2 in/12 by 12 by 5 cm high-density foam
- Felting needle
- Hot glue gun
- Hot glue sticks
- Scissors

MAKING IT YOURS
Project No. 9

LEVEL:
Easy

WHEN TO START:
3 weeks before the wedding

YIELD:
10 branches

MATERIALS
- Sand or decorative pebbles
- Ten 6-in-/15.2-cm-tall vases
- 20 branches 20 in/50.5 cm to 30 in/76.2 cm tall
- 50 to 70 artificial flower blossoms in assorted sizes and colors

TOOLS
- Hot glue gun
- Hot glue sticks

FAUX FORCED FLOWERING BRANCHES

Tap into nature's resources for these easy flowering branches. They are an attractive alternative to costly fresh flowers, add a nice height to tabletops, and can be tailored to your color palette. Look for branches with interesting twists and turns. The branch-filled vases can be top-heavy. Weighting the vases by filling them with sand or decorative pebbles will prevent them from toppling over.

HOW TO

1. **Weight the vases.** Pour sand or pebbles into each vase.

2. **Arrange the branches.** Spread the branches on a work surface. For each vase, choose two complementary branches that create a nice shape. Place the branches in the weighted vases—so you can work with the branches standing upright—by pushing them into the sand or pebbles.

3. **Add the flowers.** Working on each arrangement from bottom to top, randomly place flowers on the branches but do not glue them yet. Check the distribution of the flowers in the arrangements and make any adjustments. Using dabs of hot glue, adhere the flowers to the branches. Let dry for 10 seconds to finish.

JUTE-WRAPPED JARS

These vessels have many uses: as candleholders, vases, or containers for utensils at your buffet or straws at your bar. I recommend using jars that are at least 4 in/10 cm tall so that the webbing does not completely cover the vessels. It is nice to see the jars peeking out above or below the webbing. Well before your wedding, you can ask friends and family to gather old jars. If you don't have the sizes you need, you can purchase new canning jars to supplement.

HOW TO

1. **Measure and cut the jute webbing.** Working with one jar at a time, measure the circumference of the jar. Add ½ in/12 mm to allow for an overlap. Cut the webbing to that length. Wrap the webbing around the jar to check the fit.

2. **Cover the jars.** Run a bead of hot glue down the end of one side of the jute, from top to bottom. Wrap the other end around and press onto the glued end and hold in place for 10 seconds until the glue is set. Repeat steps 1 and 2 to cover the remaining jars.

MAKING IT YOURS
Project No. 10

LEVEL:
Easy

WHEN TO START:
4 weeks before the wedding

YIELD:
50 jars

MATERIALS
• Fifty 2- to 4-cup/480-ml to
  1-L glass jars
• 8 to 10 yd/7.3 to 9 m solid-colored
  jute upholstery webbing, 3¾ in/
  9.5 cm wide

TOOLS
• Tape measure
• Scissors
• Hot glue gun
• Hot glue sticks

STYLING IDEA

If you want to forgo the traditional floral bouquet, you have many creative alternatives to choose from: purses, parasols, large balloons, lanterns, hand fans, paper pom-poms, small wreaths, pinecones, giant prize ribbons, or pomanders made from vintage buttons and brooches. If you prefer a single bouquet, you might like one made of fabric or paper flowers, buttons, feathers, vintage jewelry, or a combination.

A Pleasant Surprise

AIRSTREAM
ELOPEMENT

Chapter No. 5

AIRSTREAM ELOPEMENT

I HAD THE HONOR OF BEING INVOLVED in planning an elopement for a sweet couple from Chattanooga, Tennessee. Their event was a great reminder of the importance of creating memories for your big day. If you are eloping, having a very small wedding, or planning on a short time line, you don't have to sacrifice style and details.

I first heard about Monica and Adam when a photographer friend shared their story with me—they wanted to elope, but they also wanted the day to be well thought out and full of memory-making details. I was a late addition to the process—let's face it, eloping usually doesn't entail a lot of planning. I quickly put together a storyboard and discussed color with the bride. After multiple e-mails, we had a plan, albeit small, since the wedding would only include the two of them and an officiant.

In many ways, I treated this wedding as a full-on event. No courthouse with ugly carpet and fluorescent lights would do for this adorable duo. They wanted to be married in a beautiful park with at least a few of the festive accouterments of a big wedding. This was my challenge.

With colors and wishes in hand, I began the design process. They had already arranged for a rickshaw to pedal them around Savannah the day of the wedding. I commissioned a graphic designer and typeface genius to paint a double-sided sign for the back of the rickshaw. One side read "We're getting married," the other "Happily ever after." I strung heart garlands with bells

from the rickshaw, so that when the couple rode away you could hear a faint jingling.

The couple had decided on the location for the wedding—one of the beautiful garden parks in the city. Ribbons quickly tossed over a low-hanging branch became the perfect bower for their nuptials. A petite square cake, two delicious Bellinis, and a half-dozen heart-shaped Rice Krispie treats on sticks greeted them after the brief ceremony.

I also had a few surprises in store. The bride loved balloons, so I tied giant white ones to a bistro bench under a moss-draped live oak tree. Behind this stood two enormous wooden initials—for the couple's names. Although this was a small-scale wedding, having these large-scale props made for memorable photographs to share with friends and family back home.

After the ceremony, they were off in the rickshaw to enjoy a ride around Savannah. When they weren't looking, I secretly tucked in a small picnic for two. The caprese sandwiches, pasta salad, and heart-shaped treat were packaged in craft paper to-go containers topped off with screen-printed wooden forks and spoons, secured with baker's twine, and accented with paper straws (a favorite of mine).

After their hour-long ride through town, Monica and Adam went to a nice restaurant close to the park where they were married. They had cocktails on the rooftop of the restaurant and dined

later in the evening. The day was very special, even with the soggy weather—yes, it rained, but you wouldn't know it from the smiles on their faces.

After their glorious Southern weekend, the couple returned home in their recently restored Airstream to share the good news with everyone. Monica told me, "They are never going to believe we decided to do this only a few weeks ago after they see how cute it all was." She was probably right, but now *you* know it can be done.

TIP

If you plan to elope or steal away for a destination wedding, you can still bring special things with you to personalize the ceremony and make it memorable. Balloons are easy to pack, and many party supply stores rent helium tanks. You can make a "just married" sign and a simple bouquet, boutonniere, and table arrangement from stems bought at a local florist. You can also order your favorite "cakelette" (perfect for two or just a few), as well as a small boxed meal for two.

GIANT LETTERS

Say it big, say it loud! Large props like these giant monograms make for fun keepsake pictures. Figure out a way to incorporate them into your day—whether you construct them yourself or find another source for the props. You can always fit the items into your home decor afterward. These letters are made from one plywood sheet that is cut in half. Some hardware stores and lumberyards will cut the sheet for you, so you can get that first big cut out of the way.

HOW TO

1. **Draw the letters.** Using the tape measure, pencil, and straightedge, mark a line widthwise down the center of the plywood, dividing it in half. Using the straightedge as a guide, draw a letter on each half of the sheet. It should fill up the allotted space. (Getting the letters perfect on the first try isn't essential, because you will later paint over any stray lines. Aim for overall balance and accurately scaled letters.)

2. **Cut out the letters.** Set up the sawhorses in a garage or outdoor workspace. Place the plywood on the sawhorses. Wearing safety goggles, use the jigsaw to cut the sheet of plywood in half, along the drawn line. Place one half on the sawhorses and

carefully cut out the letter along the lines you marked. Push the jigsaw along the lines slowly and cautiously, taking care to follow every turn. Cut the second letter.

3. **Prime the letters.** Smooth the cut edges of both letters with sandpaper. Apply a coat of primer to the front and back of the letters. Lean them against the ends of the sawhorses to dry overnight.

4. **Paint the letters.** The next day, apply paint to both sides of the letters. Let them dry overnight before moving or stacking them.

MAKING IT YOURS
Project No. 11

LEVEL:
Advanced

WHEN TO START:
4 weeks before the wedding

YIELD:
2 giant letters

MATERIALS
• One 4-by-8-ft/1.2-by-2.4-m sheet ½-in-/12-mm-thick plywood
• Primer
• Paint

TOOLS
• Tape measure
• Pencil
• Straightedge
• 2 sawhorses
• Safety goggles
• Jigsaw
• 180-grit sandpaper
• Paintbrush

LEVEL:
Easy

WHEN TO START:
1 week before the wedding

YIELD:
Picnic for 2

MATERIALS
• Food-safe paint
• 2 wooden spoons
• 2 wooden forks
• 2 deli sandwiches
• 2 side salads
• 2 food-safe craft paper containers
• Baker's twine
• 1 basket
• 2 beverages
• 2 straws
• 2 tins of candy

TOOLS
• 1 paper plate
• Brayer
• 1 decorative rubber stamp
• Scrap paper
• 1 set alphabet rubber stamps

PICNIC PACKAGING

Elopements are so romantic. Since the wedding meal will only need to serve you and your groom, you can make the details special. If you are not eloping, consider this picnic as a tidy treat to eat in the car while traveling from the ceremony to the reception. It might be the only food you will have time to savor.

HOW TO

1. **Stamp a pattern on the utensils.** Pour a small amount of paint on the paper plate. Roll the brayer through the paint, then roll a thin layer of paint on the surface of the decorative stamp. Use the scrap paper to test the stamp and to blot extra paint. Press the stamp straight down onto the back of each wooden utensil, apply even pressure, and lift the stamp straight up. Repeat to cover the utensil in an all-over pattern. Let the utensils dry for 1 hour.

2. **Stamp letters on the utensils.** Follow the same process to ink alphabet stamps and print "Mr." on the ends of one set of utensils and "Mrs." on the other. Let dry overnight.

3. **Pack the picnic.** The day beofre your ceremony, tuck the sandwiches and salads into the paper containers. Tie each container with baker's twine and secure a set of utensils to each container with a bow. Nestle the containers in a basket with the beverages, straws, and tins of candies. Store in the refrigerator until you are ready to leave.

So you decided to sneak away and get hitched, and now you are wondering how to spread the word. In this day of social media and cell phones, you can have fun sending a snapshot to surprise family and friends. You should anticipate lots of congratulatory calls and may choose to turn off your phone and have an evening to yourselves.

For a destination wedding or an elopement, you will need to research vendors in your chosen area. Most vendors have fellow professionals they prefer to work with and will gladly pass along referrals. Check them out online and read reviews. Don't be afraid to ask for references from other brides, who will happily share the names of good vendors. Images will tell you whether a vendor fits your style, but references will tell you about the vendor's work ethic.

STYLING IDEA

Use ribbons to dress up your location if you want an immediate punch of color. Ribbons are easy to hang for an instant backdrop. You can also use them to dress up a table, decorate chairs, or mark an aisle. Ribbon wands are simple to make by hot-gluing or tying strands of ribbon to the top of wooden dowels. Guests can wave them like flags for your send-off.

OLD FORT

Chapter
No. 6

OLD FORT

TRADITION LEADS MANY COUPLES to choose churches, reception halls, or hotels for their weddings. I always enjoy planning an event when a couple prefers an off-the-beaten-path location or one with historic character. Before they ever met with me, Emily and Morgan had selected the grounds of an early-nineteenth-century military fort on the outskirts of Savannah for their ceremony and reception. If you ask me, nothing signifies a strong union more than a moat, booming cannons, and sturdy fort walls!

Emily, a fashion designer, and Morgan, a photographer, saw past the obvious rusticity of the site and envisioned a day with family and friends, music, and good food. While the bride was working an internship in New York City, I met with her mother. She filled me in on a large part of Emily's vision for the wedding, so I had a good idea about what the couple wanted when I finally met with the bride. Both Emily and her mother were skilled seamstresses, which would be a huge help with many of the creative details— and a huge plus for me. Along with the design and styling of the event, my biggest challenge was bringing all the parts together into the romantic look they desired.

The bride had studied in France and was enamored of the design sense and color palette associated with the French countryside. Including those elements would soften the masculinity of the fort and give Emily the detailing she wanted. We combined Emily's love of vintage textiles and a very French color palette in shades of lavender, gray, and blue. The first project was to soften the fort's roughhewn benches. Adding fabric cushions would make the benches more comfortable and protect delicate dresses and suits from snagging on the rough wood. From burlap to vintage floral prints, we cleaned out many a fabric store. The bride's mother volunteered to sew enough seat cushions to cover fifty ceremony and reception benches. The effort was well worth it. The cushions provided a pretty, personal detail.

The initial practice run to create a wedding favor turned out to be a disaster, so we went to plan B, which resulted in an economical, easy, and practical gift. I suggested using the leftover scraps of fabric from the seat cushions to make sachets. After the bride approved, her mother stitched the sachet bags, and I filled them with French lavender and sewed them closed. The sachets were a winning last-minute replacement gift for guests.

On the day of the wedding, all eyes were on the sky. We had heard reports of severe weather for the afternoon. I was sure the weather would clear by evening, just in time for the ceremony. My confidence grew as I put together the cute directional signs outside the fort. There wasn't a cloud in the sky—in fact, it was downright hot, so hot that my staff and I took our operations under cover. We arranged the fort's long rustic tables in two rows under the open pavilion inside the fort and flanked the tables with benches. We laid muslin runners down the length of the tables and placed the cushions on the benches. Next, we rolled out two bolts of burlap and cut lengths of fabric to drape over the beams along the side of the pavilion. The cushions, runners, and draperies served to fill in and soften the pavilion space. We tied the burlap drapes back with vintage off-white cotton twill tape ribbon to create a swag effect.

The family had gathered glass containers of varying sizes and given them to a florist to use for flower arrangements. The lush and feminine blossoms struck a nice balance with the rustic nature of the surroundings. Candlelight and strings of café lights provided mood lighting. Two long pine tables were placed along either side of an alcove near the fort's entrance. As guests arrived, they signed in at one table, and as they left, they chose a favor from the opposite table. One table held a gray velvet sign-in book, an old store display with cards of congratulation clipped to it, and stacks of accordion-fold paper fans—the most-used accessory of the day. As a finishing touch for the tables, two blocks of cedar were drilled and fitted with glass test tubes, each holding a single stem of flowers. The lavender sachet favors were placed in a divided container. Vintage-style lanterns that suited the historic location flanked both tables.

The roughhewn benches presented another problem: what to do with the suit jackets that would normally be hung on chair backs? I found a picture of an old coat rack, the kind you might see in a Victorian gentlemen's club. I commissioned my furniture-designer husband to make a replica. The finished coat rack worked well and is a trick I plan to employ for future weddings. After the ceremony, we used the same area to display antique shutters hung with escort cards for the reception.

As the ceremony began, the bridesmaids and bride walked under an arch of bayonets held by soldiers in period military costume and into the fort's open field. Following the short, sweet ceremony, hors d'oeuvres and cocktails were served outdoors in the open field next to the pavilion. As unusual as this wedding was, the big surprise for guests was still to come. When the couple was announced, the costumed guards prepared a cannon, and the couple directed the firing. The night ended with sparklers and a sparkling send-off in a vintage blue convertible.

TIP *If you need coat racks for your event, you can purchase a variety of old wooden racks and paint them all the same color. The coat rack for this wedding held twelve jackets on either side. You may need multiple racks, depending on your guest list.*

WOOD-BLOCK FLOWER CENTERPIECES

This project is full of perks. The cost-saving centerpieces are versatile enough to work with modern or antique accessories. The wooden beam is bold and rustic at the same time. The aesthetic simplicity of the piece comes from the hidden glass tubes inside each hole. The test tubes can be found at stores that carry scientific equipment or stock supplies for teachers, and are available online. After the wedding, the centerpieces can be used in your home, or you can let them weather outdoors on a picnic table. The wood beam used here needs to be cut in half. The lumberyard can do this for you.

HOW TO

1. **Prepare the wood.** Using the tape measure and pencil, mark the beam so you can cut it in half crosswise. Wearing goggles and using the saw, cut the beam into two 36-in/91.5-cm pieces.

2. **Mark the beams for drilling.** With the tape measure and pencil, make a mark about 4 in/10 cm from each end of one beam. Measure between the marks and make six more marks, spacing them evenly between the marks at the ends. These marks are where you will drill each hole. Mark holes in the second beam.

3. **Drill the holes.** Fit the drill with the drill bit. Wearing the safety goggles, drill down 4 in/10 cm into a beam at each mark. Hold the drill steady and work slowly. Test the holes as you go, to make sure the test tubes will fit inside them. If not, continue working with the drill until they do. After you drill all the holes, turn the beam upside down and knock out all the bits of wood and sawdust inside the holes. Repeat to drill the second beam.

4. **Finish the wood.** Use the sandpaper to clean up the rough edges of both beams and around the drilled holes. Brush off any sawdust from the sanding. Apply the paste wax to each beam, using a cotton cloth and following the manufacturer's instructions. Work on the wax in circles and cover the whole beam. Let the wax dry for 15 minutes, then use the second cotton cloth to buff the beams.

5. **Add the flowers.** Slip a test tube into each hole. When ready to display, carefully fill the tubes with water, and then set a flower in each one.

MAKING IT YOURS
Project No. 13

LEVEL:
Moderate

WHEN TO START:
2 weeks before the wedding

YIELD:
2 centerpieces

MATERIALS
- One 6-by-6-by-72-in/15-by-15-by-183-cm rustic wood beam
- Dark paste wax
- Sixteen $5/8$-by-4-in/16-mm-by-10-cm test tubes
- 16 flowers

TOOLS
- Tape measure
- Pencil
- Safety goggles
- Chop saw or bow saw
- Electric hand drill
- $5/8$-in/16-mm drill bit
- 180-grit sandpaper
- 2 cotton cloths

ESCORT CARD DISPLAY WITH VINTAGE SHUTTERS

LEVEL:
Easy

WHEN TO START:
4 to 6 weeks before the wedding

YIELD:
1 display with 50 escort cards

MATERIALS
- Ten 8½-by-11-in/21.5-by-28-cm sheets heavy, patterned card stock
- 1 set 60-by-36-in/172-by-91-cm old hinged shutters
- 50 ornament hooks

TOOLS
- Word processing program
- Inkjet or laser printer
- Paper cutter
- Scissors
- ⅛-in/4-mm hole punch

This project provides a clever way to have guests find their tables, whether you have assigned their seats or just their table. Look for vintage shutters at flea markets, junk stores, and salvage yards. The large, dramatic shutters for this wedding were joined with hinges like a room screen and stood on their own as a feature at the wedding. You could lean a pair of shutters against a wall or place a small set on a tabletop in a zigzag formation.

HOW TO

1. **Print the tags.** Use a word processing program to lay out your guests' names and their table numbers. Choose a font that reflects your wedding style, and pick a color that complements the patterned card stock. To ensure that the text will fit on each tag, keep each line approximately 3 in/7.5 cm long. Print the tags on the card stock.

2. **Cut the tags.** With the paper cutter, cut tags 2½ in/6 cm tall by 4 in/10 cm wide. Use the grid and ruler on the edge of the paper cutter to keep the cuts aligned. Snip the top corners off each tag with scissors. Punch a hole in the top of each tag, positioning it ¼ in/6 mm from the top edge and centering it between the cut corners.

3. **Set up the shutters.** Stand the shutters upright. Insert a hook into the hole on each tag, then hang on a slat of the shutter. Arrange the tags alphabetically, so guests can easily find their names.

LAVENDER SACHETS

Put those leftover scraps of fabric from other wedding projects to good use for these lavender-filled sachets. They are elegant, romantic, and useful favors. Lavender flower buds are easy to find in bulk, but for a twist, think about filling yours with dried rose petals or a variety of dried herbs.

HOW TO

1. **Cut the scraps.** Lay the fabric on a flat surface. Measure and cut one hundred 5-in/12-cm squares. Use the pinking shears to give them a decorative edge. Select scraps with matching patterns and stack them in pairs, with the right sides facing out.

2. **Sew the sachets.** Align the pieces of the first pair of fabric scraps, and stitch three sides closed, using a ¼-in/6-mm seam allowance. Sew along 3 in/7.5 cm of the fourth side, leaving a 2-in/5-cm opening. Repeat to sew 50 sachets.

3. **Fill the sachets.** Insert the funnel into the opening of each sachet. Fill with ½ cup/20 g lavender buds. Sew the opening closed to seal the sachet.

LEVEL:
Easy

WHEN TO START:
2 weeks before the wedding

YIELD:
50 sachets

MATERIALS
- Fabric scraps at least 5 in/12 cm wide
- 2 lb/910 g dried lavender buds

TOOLS
- Tape measure
- Pinking shears
- Sewing machine
- Thread
- Wide-mouth funnel
- Measuring cup

STYLING IDEA

Adding textiles is one of the easiest and most cost-effective ways to embellish a venue. If your event takes place in a rustic building or a tent, use fabric to mask off an unsightly area or enhance a particularly pretty aspect of the location. You can also hang lengths of fabric to delineate the head table, make a backdrop for photos or the ceremony itself, frame the cake table, or decorate a chuppah.

TIP *Rather than direct guests to a particular seat, you can direct them to a table to encourage mingling. Guests find their way to the table number on their escort card and then choose their own seats. You can assign seats or tables, depending on how friendly your family and friends are with each other.*

Good signage is an often overlooked necessity for weddings. Whether you place signs on the roadside or just outside your event, you will need directional signs indicating where to turn and park, the location of restrooms, and the destinations for pertinent activities. Sign painters or artisans can create graphics or vinyl letters that match the look of your invitations. There are also terrific online resources for custom-designed signs.

FLEA MARKET CHARM

Chapter No. 7

FLEA MARKET CHARM

THE BRIDE AND GROOM ARE FROM VIRGINIA, but they adored Charleston, South Carolina, and dreamed of a Southern wedding under grand old oak trees. If they held the wedding back home, the whole town would want to be invited—they knew just about everyone. The solution was to plan a big party in Virginia after the honeymoon and keep the Charleston wedding an intimate affair. They selected a rustic carriage house on the property of an eighteenth-century plantation home on the banks of the Ashley River.

The moment the bride, Ashley (a coincidence!), walked through the door for our first meeting, I knew we would make a good team. I could tell she was a modern woman who also loved vintage things. Dressed in layered, lacy clothes and a fedora, and wearing clever, retro shoes, she was toting an old suitcase, which I soon discovered was filled with magical bits of antiques and images that were the inspiration for the look and feel of the wedding.

As we dove into conversation and poured the contents of the suitcase onto the table, I got an idea of what would be her color palette. She adored shades of parchment, beige, and gray—but pink was the most prominent color. Ashley wanted a soft, faded pink, the kind found in worn-out curtains that used to be red but have been bleached by the sun to the perfect shade of pink. She was speaking my language—fabric that is faded and worn, with a hint of history.

Charleston had many terrific resources for vintage decor but not at a price that we were eager to pay. Rather than give up some of her ideas, I did some research and a little fancy wedding math (moving expenditures around to make the most of her priorities). I thought that we could get the look she wanted with some footwork and ingenuity. The carriage house had no banquet tables and chairs for dining, so everything had to be brought in. We rented tables, chairs, linen, and cocktail tables—the basics. She needed to buy or borrow a sign-in table filled with unique props, a favor table for the guests, a cake table, and a few other things that she didn't want to rent.

Next we wrote a shopping list and took stock of the items we already had. Both Ashley and her mother were flea market and estate sale aficionados. We quickly realized that, among us, we had a few farm tables, a giant bulletin board, old suitcases, blue Ball jars, and other decorative odds and ends. What she really wanted was mismatched antique china with hints of her color palette and a long doily runner for the bridal party table.

I scoured flea markets, estate sales, thrift stores, and auctions in Georgia, and they did the same in Virginia and neighboring Ohio. We all searched online and managed to find enough dinner and bread and butter plates for the seated dinner and cake afterward—for less than the price of rental tableware! We kept a running tabulation of what we had purchased via weekly e-mail updates. I will never forget Ashley and her mother

Having a destination wedding will reduce your head count because invitees are not always willing or able to travel. If you pick a popular, accessible destination, you are likely to have better attendance. If you want to keep the number of guests low, choose a small, remote location. Most people understand when you tell them that you're planning an intimate wedding with only a few guests.

confessing to me what a great time they had seeking out these special items. Ashley had to rent a trailer to bring her collectibles to the wedding. Some of the dishes and antiques now share space with the other antiques in her home. After the wedding, the couple chose their favorites for a set of starter china and sold the rest.

To make a head table for the bridal party, I placed banquet tables end to end, creating enough space to seat twenty-two people. I covered the table with floor-length cloths and topped it with a handmade runner. The runner, a big money saver and an attractive keepsake, was fashioned from more than a hundred vintage doilies in varying shades and sizes that we had collected.

The wedding was held outdoors on the bank of the Ashley River. After the ceremony, cocktails were served on the terrace and just inside the carriage house. We placed the escort cards for seating and the sign-in table in the cocktail area, and created a transitional divide between the areas by draping panels of fabric in the doorways. After cocktails, I pulled the drapes back to reveal the dining area, and guests found their seats.

When your ceremony and reception are in close proximity, it is important to divide time and space efficiently. After cocktails, guests tend to find their chairs, park their purses, and take off their jackets. My personal preference is for the newlywed couple to make their entrance and begin the evening with everyone seated—or at least paying attention. In this case, I wanted to create boundaries that would help guide guests through the evening so that each element had its own place and time.

Instead of the usual bride and groom's cake, the couple chose a small, two-tiered cake for themselves and cupcakes for their guests—an economical and adorable alternative to a large cake. Mismatched bread and butter plates from the sets of flea market china were used for the cupcakes. A vintage cake tin served as a stand for the cutting cake.

A venue with an established decor may not fit the style and look you want for your wedding. On the other hand, using an unfurnished venue means that you have to rent or purchase items for your event. Budget considerations should be taken into account, but having an unfinished venue gives you an opportunity to create your own vision. You can save money by borrowing items from family and friends, or by shopping for affordable antiques that you can use in your home after the ceremony.

If you have plenty of time and like to shop flea markets and antique stores—and you aren't afraid of the occasional box of dirty dishes with cobwebs—plan to purchase your own vintage china for the reception. Establish a limit for how much you will pay for each piece, but expect to pay a little more here and there if certain items are especially nice. You can always sell the pieces online afterward if you choose not to keep them.

I crafted the cake topper from millinery flowers, vintage papers, an antique porcelain bride and groom, and glittery pieces of vintage jewelry, all affixed to an old tin lid from one of the bride's blue Ball jars.

Vintage details were in abundance throughout this wedding. The guests' favors were paperweights, collages in a pink palette using vintage papers and old engravings. The table centerpieces were stacks of old books, topped with old medicine bottles and jars holding flowers and mercury glass votive holders. I brought along old sheet music—I had grabbed a stack at random from my collection—and when the sheets were laid out to decorate the cake table, they all turned out to be wedding music. A very happy accident!

BRIDAL SONG.

COLLAGE PAPERWEIGHTS

The level of detail required for this project makes it ideal for small weddings where you can customize the favors for your guests. Each paperweight becomes a miniature work of art. The kits are simple and would be a fun activity for a crafty bridal shower. Set out paperweight kits and ephemera and let each guest at the shower create a collage or two.

HOW TO

1. **Create the collages.** Let your creativity guide you, and look for colors and patterns from the ephemera that inspire you. Combine old advertisements or letters with a millinery leaf and then top off the combination with an old button. When you are pleased with each collage, use the glue stick to adhere the elements together.

2. **Attach the collages to the mounting boards.** For each paperweight, remove the backing from the adhesive mounting board provided in the kit. Place the collage on the mounting board. Use scissors to trim any overhanging parts of the collage from the board.

3. **Finish the paperweights.** Fit the mounting board into the recess in the base of each glass paperweight. Remove the backing from the adhesive of the bottom pad, center it on the bottom of the paperweight, and press it firmly in place.

MAKING IT YOURS
Project No. 16

LEVEL:
Easy

WHEN TO START:
4 to 6 weeks before the wedding

YIELD:
50 paperweights

MATERIALS
- Vintage ephemera such as letters, advertisements, ribbons, buttons, patterned tape, millinery flowers and leaves
- 50 paperweight kits in a variety of shapes

TOOLS
- Glue stick
- Scissors

LEVEL:
Easy

WHEN TO START:
3 weeks before the wedding

YIELD:
One 28-ft/8.5-m runner

MATERIALS
• Seventy-five 3-in/7.5-cm to 10-in/ 25-cm round vintage doilies

TOOLS
• Butcher paper
• Needle
• Coordinating thread
• One 48-in-/122-cm-long cardboard tube (optional)

DOILY RUNNER

This pretty white table runner is simultaneously delicate and dramatic. Dozens of intricate doilies are connected into an impressive piece. If you will be using round tables, just work the doilies into a circle instead of a runner. The handmade treasures are common finds at thrift stores, but to add deep meaning and personalize the runner, consider incorporating a doily or two from a loved one.

HOW TO

1. **Arrange the doilies.** To help manage the oversized length of this project, make seven small sections and join them together. Lay the butcher paper on your work surface. Cover it with as many doilies as you can arrange without overlapping their edges. Work the large doilies in first, then fill in the gaps with the smaller doilies.

2. **Sew the doilies.** Sew the edges of the doilies together with a needle and thread. Work gently with the delicate material. Repeat to make six more sections.

3. **Sew the sections together.** Align the edges of two sections and sew them together. Repeat to attach the remaining five sections.

4. **Roll the runner.** If desired, roll the runner around the cardboard tube as you sew the sections together. Keep the runner on the tube for storage and transportation. On the day of the event, unroll the runner onto your table.

A cake stand doesn't need to be in a traditional style. Pick an unusual object to display your cake and remember to give the baker either the dimensions or the actual stand, so that the cake will fit perfectly. With any antique, make sure the stand is clean and sanitary, or use a decorative paper or fabric buffer between the cake and the stand.

STYLING IDEA

For interesting centerpieces, stack old books, small wooden crates, antique boxes, or drawers to elevate your floral arrangements to different levels. To complement these items, supply your florist with antique and vintage vases and containers. Finally, add lots of sparkly votive candles to light the table. You don't need to make every table look the same. The overall effect will be more engaging if the centerpieces have variety.

FARMHOUSE
FETE

FARMHOUSE FETE

WHEN HOLLY, AN ASSISTANT PRINT DESIGNER for Lilly Pulitzer, came to me for help with her wedding, I was very excited. I first met Holly when she was attending art school, and she later worked in my store, so I was very familiar with her style, her love of vintage goods, and her skill at making beautiful objects.

At our initial meeting we sat across the table from each other facing piles of inspirational images, doodles of things she wanted to make, swatches of fabric, and a list of wishes and needs for the big day. She could see that my mind was reeling with possibilities and quickly reminded me of her conservative budget. She made it very clear that a lot of items would have to be handmade or found at a reasonable price, such as at flea markets. Because her expectation was for a casual celebration with family and friends in an outdoor setting, I knew we could make the day beautiful within her budget. Armed with this information and knowing I had a partner in crime when it came to collecting vintage wares, I had no doubt we could achieve the look she wanted.

Holly wasn't shy about the colors she liked. She wanted to include several shades of orange, ranging from bright to soft peach, and a spectrum of green, from citron to moss. She shared the shades of orange with her bridesmaids and encouraged them to select dresses in any of those shades. This worked beautifully—they were able to choose something they actually liked and would wear again.

Once the palette was established, our discussion focused on the feel for the day. Holly wanted a wedding with a simple, casual atmosphere filled with Southern character. Since the venue would play a big part of creating that feeling, we talked about options near her hometown of Salisbury, North Carolina. Holly and her fiancé, Daniel, had already decided that their hometown Catholic church would be the perfect place for the ceremony. For the reception, they wanted a unique location. At first they considered a local train depot for its proximity to the church and town, but after much deliberation Holly, Daniel, and Holly's mother extended their search beyond Salisbury. They were pleasantly surprised to find an 1829 farmhouse forty-five minutes from the church.

The white clapboard farmhouse was situated on a rolling lawn with a barn and flanked by woods on one side and bamboo on the other. The shade would be a welcome feature, since the reception was a midday affair in June—usually a hot, steamy time of year. She wanted Southern character, and nothing says Southern character better than heat!

The venue was a blank slate that we could build upon. The farmhouse had pine clapboard walls and simple warm wood floors. The front and back lawn was a lush green, and the large old tree branches hung low overhead. The uninterrupted view from the white rockers on the front porch was of a sunlit cornfield that proved to be a gem of a backdrop for the bridal portraits.

To set the tone for their wedding, the couple sent out screen-printed fabric save-the-dates that included a sheer layer with the wording and a thicker layer with a decorative border Holly had designed. The save-the-dates hung from a small raffia handle so guests could keep them in plain sight. The design incorporated some of the decorative elements Holly used in the invitations, programs, and maps. Holly, a gifted textile designer, created her own pattern for many of the paper and textile items used throughout the wedding. Not every bride has the ability or resources to create her designs and have fabric printed, but using interesting fabrics or patterns is an easy way to stretch your decorating budget and still make a lot of impact. Your local fabric store can be a stellar source of inspiration.

For her special day, Holly chose a simple dress and dolled it up with a stunning vintage necklace, a sash with a soft fabric flower, and sweet flats in a shade of coral. Adding touches of color or a little sparkle can enhance a simple wedding dress. The groom and groomsmen wore light beige suits with boutonnieres that Holly made from vintage flower pins and floral fabric of her own design. In lieu of live flowers, Holly and her bridesmaids carried handcrafted glass-beaded bouquets—a centuries-old European tradition expertly reproduced by the bride's mother. It was a big endeavor for this self-taught beader to create not one bridal bouquet but seven extraordinary bouquets. She was up for the challenge because she knew the beaded blossoms would be lasting mementos for Holly and her bridesmaids.

Guests arriving at the reception were directed to the front lawn of the farmhouse to enjoy punch and hors d'oeuvres. The historic home was open for guests to explore. To avoid a hot-summer wedding-cake meltdown, we displayed the cake in the front parlor until it was time for the traditional cake cutting. We also wanted everyone to see the cake topper Holly had made: a needle-felted bride and groom atop a round box adorned with notions and yarn. The couple arrived shortly after cocktails had begun and were greeted with a happy roar from the crowd.

All the guests made their way toward the barn for dinner and dancing. Before they found their seats, guests needed to sign in at a photo booth. Using an instant film camera, guests each took their own pictures and wrote a message for the couple on the photo. They then positioned the images on a floral-patterned card. The cards were clipped to petite wire hangers and hung on three clotheslines strung between tall tomato stakes. The installation was next to the sign-in table. As guests walked in to dinner, they could read the messages on the way to their tables. At the end of the evening, I presented the bride and groom with a pretty ribbon-tied bundle of the cards as a keepsake.

Fifteen long, narrow dining tables were covered with off-white, floor-length cloths and topped with simple brown butcher paper and 1940s restaurant dinnerware. The mismatched napkins were made from vintage-inspired fabrics that fit the color palette.

TIP

To designate seats for the newlyweds at the reception, tie vintage paper bells to the backs of their chairs. You can also achieve the same attention-getting effect with ribbons, signs, or their initials.

The tables were left unadorned in preparation for a family-style dinner for 150 guests. Each dish was brought out in waxed paper–lined baskets and bowls and passed around the table. For this reason, we decided to forgo centerpieces, which would have made the table too crowded for this casual style of dining.

Following dinner, people made their way to the hay bales laid about the property to relax or play board games, horseshoes, badminton, and cards, or they wandered back to the photo booth for a more festive photo session after a few cocktails. The band got the crowd going by playing Southern classics as the cake was carried to the front of the barn. The cake table, a family heirloom, showcased the cake beautifully.

At the end of the celebration, just before storm clouds rolled in, guests sent the newlyweds off amid a sea of bubbles while music played in the background. As the guests left to go home, they were presented with little jars of homemade jam with customized labels to commemorate the day.

TIP

Holding your reception a long distance from the location of the ceremony can be both a burden and a blessing. You have to plan transportation for you and, possibly, your guests; provide maps; and build the travel time into your schedule. But the extra time between the ceremony and the reception is a big plus because it gives you and your groom a respite and a chance to enjoy each other's company before the following festivities.

JAM FAVORS

Look at your wedding favors as an opportunity to share part of your life and your family history with guests. In this case, the jam might be made from your favorite fruit or produce from your best friend's orchard. Using a treasured family recipe for the preserves is a wonderful way to honor your loved ones. Edible favors are guaranteed crowd pleasers, but you don't have to be a dedicated cook to make these pretty jars of jam. Although the jam for this wedding was homemade, you can save time and still offer a charming favor by using a high-quality store-bought or local product. A rusty vintage wire rack would be the perfect display for these pretty jam jars.

HOW TO

1. **Sterilize the jars.** Wash and dry the jars, lids, and screw bands. Fill the pot with water and bring to a simmer. Working in batches if necessary, immerse the jars, without their lids and bands, in the simmering water. Remove with tongs and set on a clean surface.

2. **Fill the jars.** Use a large spoon to fill each jar with the jam, leaving a ¼-in/ 6-mm headspace. Assemble a lid and screw band and tightly screw onto the jar.

3. **Boil the jars.** Bring the water in the pot to a boil. Using the tongs, lower a few jars at a time into the boiling water. Be sure the jars are completely covered with the boiling water and that they don't touch each other or the sides of the pot. Boil the jars for 10 minutes to seal them. Remove with the tongs and set aside to cool for 24 hours.

4. **Check the seals.** When the jars start to cool, you will hear the lids pop as they retract. After the jars have cooled, press each lid with a finger to make sure it is depressed. If a lid depresses but then pops back up, the jar is not adequately sealed. Refrigerate that jar and use the jam immediately, rather than save it for your wedding.

5. **Label the jars.** Compose a message for the labels and select a pretty font. Use a word processing program or the template provided by the label manufacturer to format the text. Print the labels on your printer. Affix a label to the center of each lid.

MAKING IT
YOURS
Project No. 18

LEVEL:
Moderate

WHEN TO START:
6 weeks before the wedding if using homemade jam

YIELD:
Fifty ½-pint/240-ml jars

MATERIALS
- Fifty ½-pint/240-ml Ball jars with lids and screw bands
- 12½-qt/12-L store-bought or homemade jam
- Fifty 2½-in/6-cm round self-adhesive labels for home printing

TOOLS
- Large pot
- Tongs
- Large spoon
- Word processing program or label printing templates
- Laser or inkjet printer

LEVEL:
Easy

WHEN TO START:
1 week before the wedding

YIELD:
10 bowls and 10 baskets

MATERIALS

- Ten 10-in/25-cm-diameter clear acrylic bowls
- Ten 10-in/25-cm-diameter plastic food serving baskets
- 2 cans multipurpose spray paint
- Patterned waxed paper in variety of colors

TOOLS

- Drop cloth
- Respirator
- Scissors

WAXED PAPER BOWLS AND BASKETS

If you choose a family-style dinner service, your tables may not have enough space for both the centerpieces and the food. One solution is to create these colorful bowls and baskets. Elevate them above the ordinary by lining them with equally colorful patterned waxed paper. Presentation is everything, and these containers will make the tables and the food look festive.

HOW TO

1. **Prepare your workspace.** Choose a well-ventilated space for painting that has good light and is free of dust and debris. Lay a drop cloth down to keep the space clean.

2. **Paint the bowls and baskets.** Set the bowls and baskets face-down on the drop cloth. (If working with two colors, put half of the bowls and baskets aside and paint them separately.) Shake a spray can for 2 minutes to mix the paint. Wearing the respirator, hold the can 12 in/30.5 cm away from the vessels and apply the paint in thin layers, using even, swooping motions. By moving the can as you spray, you are less likely to create drips. After applying the first coat, let the paint dry for 20 minutes. If necessary, apply a second coat. Let the bowls and baskets stand for 24 hours to cure completely. Repeat to spray the remaining bowls and baskets with the second color.

3. **Line the bowls.** When ready to fill, cut the waxed paper, and line each bowl and basket with one or two sheets.

STYLING IDEA

A photo booth is a terrific way to get guests up and out of their seats. People are more likely to cut up and do things they wouldn't normally do under the watchful eye of the wedding photographer. The booth is simple to set up. You can hang ribbons, a length of fabric, or a sign as a backdrop. Provide an instant film camera, replacement film, and some fun props, and you are ready to go.

TIP

Choosing family-style dining won't necessarily lower your costs. Additional china may need to be rented because many dishes are laid out on each table and shared among guests. You will still want help bringing the dishes to the table, and you will need to keep food warm. Your caterer can come up with creative options for a menu that will work family style. If your budget is limited, choose a simple buffet or food stations, popular options that reduce rental and labor expenses.

You can find color inspiration everywhere but never as convenient and practical as at a local paint or hardware store. When choosing your palette, look at paint chips in your favorite colors along with related shades that are brighter and lighter.

Lovely Day

Lovely Day

WHO AND HOW MANY TO INVITE to your wedding are always tough questions for you and your groom. I like to remind couples that a wedding should be shared with those who mean the most to them. Whether you invite two hundred guests or only twenty, the decision is ultimately yours. The "bigger is better" attitude sometimes results in losing sight of the real meaning of a wedding. A small wedding can bring cost savings and, as an additional benefit, can help alleviate the guilt of not inviting a long list of family members and acquaintances.

When Amy and Josh told me they wanted a fun, intimate occasion for forty guests—more like a picnic than a huge ceremony—I was pleased to work with their vision. Because the event would be small, a private home would work for both the ceremony and the party. Amy wanted a waterfront locale for the ceremony with a sprawling yard to accommodate a day filled with games and a picnic lunch for family and friends.

Locations like these are hard to come by for several reasons. If you find a private home that suits your event, parking, restrooms, and neighborhood restrictions all need to be considered. Parking and restrooms are the easiest to address. You can shuttle guests from a central location and arrange fancy potties through a rental company. The last issue, neighborhood restrictions, can be tough. Make sure your hosts have cleared the event with

their neighborhood association or other appropriate entity long before your big day. You don't want to be forced to make last-minute changes.

Because Amy and Josh didn't know of a home that would work for their wedding, I approached a friend who had rented her lovely residence and gardens to film crews. After all, this wedding would be a much smaller affair than a film production. She said yes, and I brought the couple to meet her and see the home. As it turned out, they knew each other, which made the process much more comfortable.

With the location secured, the fun of planning began. The bride shared her love of hot air balloons, so I suggested that we include this imagery in her picnic paper goods and accessories. I commissioned a local boutique owner to embroider tiny hot air balloons on handkerchiefs for both the bride and the groom. The men's boutonnieres crafted by another artisan were hot air balloons as well and were inspired by the same embroidery design.

Amy's cheerful, lighthearted palette included the hues found in the colorful stripes of hot air balloons—reds, yellows, blues, pinks. For her bouquet, the bride wanted to add some whimsy, so I made giant pink crepe paper peonies, wrapped them together, and finished them with ribbon. They were the perfect complement to the pink satin sash on her dress. If you have the time to make paper flowers, they are an inexpensive alternative to real flowers. You can also use paper flowers for your table centerpieces. You will want to start early and even recruit friends to help. Keep in mind that outdoor climates can affect the texture of paper flowers. If humidity will be a concern at your location, and you still want an alternative to fresh flowers, you can opt for flowers made of starched fabric.

For the ceremony, we lined up chairs facing the water, and a friend crafted a fun backdrop and fabric aisle decorations. The bride wore a short seersucker wedding dress, the groom a simple white shirt, a handmade vest, and a bow tie paired with taupe slacks. Groomsmen wore white shirts with suspenders and bow ties given to them by the couple (made and embroidered at the same stitch shop as the handkerchiefs). The hot air balloon boutonnieres finished off their attire. The bridesmaids wore their own vintage dresses in an array of colors related to Amy's color palette. She liked that each was able to show her personality, and she knew her bridesmaids so well that she was certain that they would pick cute dresses.

TIP

Many local craft stores and crafters can make wonderful items that you can include in your wedding. They are often more reasonable and more personal than store-bought products. When you commission handcrafts, you can often customize them by including pieces of jewelry or fabric from a family heirloom such as your mother's wedding dress or hair piece. You could also stitch charms, trinkets, or souvenirs from a special place to your ring bearer's pillow or your slip. Only you will know that the treasure is there, but the meaning will be dear.

After the ceremony, guests were directed to the picnic area with a pink handmade sign. Each couple was handed a picnic basket marked with both a numbered tag designating their blanket or table and a little felted drumstick or carrot (the latter to signify it was a vegetarian meal). We served raspberry lemonade and sweet tea in decorative glasses atop little cocktail napkins made from mismatched fabric within the color palette.

Music played in the background but wasn't the focus of the day. Games were more important to this couple and fit the backyard ambiance they wanted. A local letterpress company created tabletop games like connect the dots and tic-tac-toe, and guests young and old enjoyed their old-fashioned appeal. Guests could play lawn games, too—both badminton and bocce ball. As people lingered on blankets, they enjoyed cookies, tarts, marshmallow pops, and pie.

The newlyweds prefer pie to cake, so they knew it would be a fitting alternative for their big day. I created a pair of pie birds for their topper. A long white farm table on the lawn held the sweet treats. Vintage table tents from an estate sale kept the insects at bay. One was adorned with tiny chenille bugs—an accidental touch of whimsy.

Amy and Josh wanted to give something personal to guests. Months before their wedding, they had started rooting succulents in their garden. By the time the wedding rolled around, they had enough plants for everyone. We potted them in tiny baskets that matched the picnic theme and decorated each basket with miniature tissue paper flowers. The guests were presented with baskets as they departed. These lovely little mementos would continue to grow and not be put away in a drawer.

This wedding was one of those lazy, easy days filled with love, laughter, and friendship.

CREPE PAPER BOUQUET

Do you want a particular flower that isn't in season for your ceremony? Do you like the idea of playing with scale? Or perhaps you just want to have a bouquet that you can keep long after the big day. Paper flowers fit the bill every time and can be made in any size and color.

HOW TO

1. **Set up your work area.** Choose a work surface in a well-ventilated area, and cover the surface with butcher paper.

2. **Cut and spray the paper.** While the crepe paper is still folded, cut a 6-in/15-cm wide piece from the bottom. Keep this piece folded, and cut along the cut edge to replicate the curves along the top of a flower petal. Unfold the paper and cut the strip to 72 in/183 cm long. Repeat to cut five more strips and then lay them flat on your work surface. Wearing rubber gloves, shake the can of paint well and lightly spray the bottom 2 in/5 cm of the straight edge of each strip. Set aside for 5 minutes to dry.

3. **Make the blossoms.** Apply a dab of hot glue to the end of one floral wire. With the darkened side of the paper facing in, attach the edge of one end of the crepe paper strip to the wire stem. Turn the wire and gather the strip around the stem to form a flower. Apply a dab of glue to the inside of the end of the strip and press it down to hold the blossom together. Let the glue dry for 10 seconds. Repeat to form five more blossoms. Ruffle the edges of the petals to make each blossom look lush. Then, working from the outside of each blossom, gently tug the edge of the paper to add curves and widen each petal.

4. **Make the bouquet.** Gather the wire stems together and wrap them with the floral tape. Set the taped wires on the stick and wrap together with floral tape to create a stem to finish.

MAKING IT YOURS
Project No. 20

LEVEL:
Easy

WHEN TO START:
1 week before the wedding

YIELD:
1 bouquet

MATERIALS
- Two 20-by-90-in/50-by-229-cm crepe paper folds
- 1 can floral spray paint, one shade darker than crepe paper
- Six 12-in/30.5-cm floral wire stems
- Brown floral tape
- One 6-in/15-cm wooden stick from your yard

TOOLS
- Butcher paper
- Scissors
- Tape measure
- Rubber gloves
- Hot glue gun
- Hot glue sticks

LEVEL:
Easy

WHEN TO START:
1 week before the wedding

YIELD:
2 signs

MATERIALS
• 4 white heavyweight paper coasters
• 2 cupcake liners with scalloped
 edges
• 2 wooden skewers

TOOLS
• 1 set alphabet rubber stamps
• Ink pad
• Hot glue gun
• Hot glue sticks

SWEET LOVE SIGNS

These cute ruffled signs can be made in just a few minutes. The versions shown here denote both the contents of the drinks and the feeling for the day. They could just as easily be used on a sweets table or with the cake. They are so appealing that you shouldn't be surprised if guests commandeer them for props while posing for photos.

HOW TO

1. **Stamp the coasters.** Choose two words, one for each sign, that are short enough to fit onto the center of two coasters without crowding the letters. Press each stamp into the ink pad to coat it with ink. Press it directly and firmly down on the coaster. Lift it straight up, to avoid smears. Re-ink the stamp before every use. You will only need to stamp one side of each coaster.

2. **Layer and glue the signs.** Flatten the cupcake liners. Center one of the coasters on a cupcake paper so that the scallops peek out around the edge. Glue the paper in place on the back of the coaster. Let dry for at least 10 seconds. Glue the skewer to the back of the second coaster and let dry for at least 10 seconds. Sandwich the two coasters back to back and glue them together. Let the sign dry for at least 10 seconds. Repeat to create the second sign.

STYLING IDEA

A cake table is a fun place to show off your personal style. You can decorate the table with banners, bunting, or garlands, and choose interesting stands and servers, whether your menu includes a single cake, several pies, or an array of cupcakes. The cake (or pie) topper doesn't have to be the traditional bride and groom and can say something about you as a couple.

TIP

Hosting a wedding at home is not necessarily easier or less expensive than holding a ceremony and reception at another location. You will likely need to rent a tent, tables, chairs, and linens, and hire servers, to name some of the basics. Unless you plan a small event (fewer than fifty guests), you should consider a site that can best fulfill all your needs and accommodate your guest count, and can provide a dedicated staff to see that your wedding runs smoothly.

If you want to save on catering costs, you could host a daytime ceremony and reception. Lunch menus are often less expensive and less time-consuming for caterers. A daytime event also offers an opportunity to be playful with the menu. Think about having an ice-cream or cotton-candy cart on site in the summer or a soup station in the fall or winter.

REPORT CARD

Date

Deliver To

garding

Acknowledge Receipt

SCHOOLHOUSE ROCK

Chapter
No. 10

SCHOOLHOUSE ROCK

WHAT DO YOU GET WHEN a beautiful Latina schoolteacher marries a good-looking, long-haired Southern welder with rock star looks? A wonderfully diverse mix of guests, music, food, and styles. When Jazmin and I first discussed her wedding, she told me that she was more concerned about the overall feel of the event than the small details. She already had a color scheme and knew what she wanted for the cake and the flowers. My job was to pull all her must-haves together into a wedding that felt effortless and would reflect their personalities.

I frequently ask brides to share images that inspire them—but not necessarily images of other weddings. You can do this when planning your event. Look closely at the clothes and interiors you like, and think about how you and your fiancé live. This will give you clues about your preferred colors and other elements that can be incorporated into your decor. This information is more important than dozens of pictures of cakes and centerpieces from other weddings. Jazmin had saved a magazine photo of a girl wearing a golden yellow twin set with a gray pencil skirt. She loved the gray paired with a happier tone. That classic image, vintage in a *Mad Men* sort of way, became the touchstone for making color and fabric selections.

Compared to the desires of most brides, Jazmin's were quite simple: she wanted a wedding that literally represented her and Charles as a couple. By literal, she meant that both of their

professions—welding and teaching—should be reflected in the festivities. I envisioned using graph paper, flash cards, teacher's bells, chalkboards, and pencils, but bringing the groom's welder world into the mix would prove a little harder.

We found a stationery designer who would be able to capture the two of them on paper. The wedding invitation featured silhouettes of the couple flanked by tools of their trade, similar to an old-fashioned advertisement. One corner showed a welder's helmet, an arc, a toolbox, and gloves; in the opposite corner were books, a ruler, and an apple. The invitation set the tone for the entire event in both color and theme.

When choosing a venue for the late summer ceremony, Charles remembered visiting the ruins of an old church with his parents when he was a child. The Old Sheldon Ruins near Beaufort, South Carolina, is the site of a Greek Revival church that was burned first during the Revolutionary War, then was rebuilt and burned again during the Civil War. The picturesque ruins with spectacular brick columns and arches, set among majestic old oaks, are a popular site for visitors. Charles and Jazmin were awed by the beauty and history and chose to be married in this magical place. But the location was nearly an hour's drive from the reception site and lacked facilities. With no remaining roof, the ruins were essentially an outdoor venue. We knew we might have to contend with the weather.

Because the ceremony was going to be brief, guests would stand instead of sit. To delineate an aisle, a pathway was lined with ribbons strung from stakes. Otherwise, people would have a tendency to crowd around the couple, making it difficult for the photographer to have a view of the ceremony and for the couple to exit.

The bride and attendants arrived shortly before 5:30 P.M. and awaited their cue to walk the path to the ceremony. Dressed in gray, the bridesmaid and man of honor (yes, man of honor) stepped from the car first, and then Jazmin appeared wearing a short, sparkly 1950s-style dress with cap sleeves, high-high heels, and a sweet cage veil. As the ceremony ended, I rang a giant teacher's bell, since the church did not have bells. Dark clouds quickly rolled in, so guests rushed to their cars and went to the reception while the bridal party took advantage of the time alone to have pictures taken around the historic site. When the photo session came to a close, the newlyweds hopped into a spiffy 1960s black Cadillac and drove down the long tree-lined road toward their reception.

TIP

You may forgo seating if your ceremony is short and sweet, but do provide a few creature comforts. Ice water, paper parasols, and fans are welcome extras to have on hand to ensure the comfort of your guests.

Unless you are a stickler for tradition, don't be afraid to ask your best male friend to be "man of honor" on your side of the altar. Just because your best friend is a man doesn't mean he has to be excluded from your big day.

Thankfully, all the guests arrived at the reception before the worst of the rain started. Just inside the entrance, they wrote messages to the newlyweds on old-fashioned sentence strips, the kind with a dotted line between two solid lines. The messages went into a wire in-and-out bin similar to those found on a teacher's desk. An old-timey chalkboard on an oak stand, placed beside the sign-in table, served as an entertaining backdrop for an instant photo booth. People chose from a supply of school and welding props for their photos. Many took the opportunity to write advice to the couple on the blackboard and act out silly scenarios for the keepsake photos, which were deposited in a metal tin for the couple to enjoy later.

"La Vie en Rose" played as the newlyweds were announced and stepped onto the dance floor for their first dance. As it turns out, this was the song that the bride's ninety-four-year-old grandmother had danced to at her wedding. Jazmin had not known this and had chosen the music because she loved it. The coincidence was a good omen and a nice surprise to share with her grandmother.

The dining and cocktail tables were decorated with mixed containers of flowers and candles atop charcoal gray linens. The couple had a space of their own, an antique pedestal table with yellow chairs marked "bride" and "groom," set close to the dance floor so they didn't miss a thing. Enormous paper chains fashioned from the same sentence strips used for the sign-in table, hung on the DJ table and food station tables and around the chalkboard, made a festive addition to the decor.

The bride wanted people to enjoy sweets throughout the night rather than wait for her to cut a traditional wedding cake. Her favorite cookies and candies sat on trays and in pretty jars surrounding the wedding cake. Using scoops and glassine bags, guests could serve themselves. A smaller chalkboard to one side of the dessert table provided a clever key to the sweets on the table, much like the insert in a box of chocolates. The cookies and candies were in a range of yellow shades. A bright yellow lamp sat on either end of the table.

To round out the night, the DJ played a great mix of vintage Latin dance music and the couple's favorites, and by the night's end the entire crowd was on the dance floor.

The lesson you can learn from this charming wedding is that you and your groom can have a lot of fun when you explore the lighthearted side of your professions.

TIP *You and your groom will want time alone at your wedding. Having a table of your own is one way to steal a few moments to yourselves. Designate a small table and two chairs marked with your names or signs saying "Bride" and "Groom," or "Mr." and "Mrs." You will always have a seat—and a bit of privacy.*

GIANT PAPER CHAIN

For this wedding, a small paper chain would have been lost in such a large space. You can use large sentence strips to make an oversized chain appropriate for a large-scale venue.

HOW TO

Make and link the paper rings. With the printed lines facing out, bend a strip into a loop. Staple the ends together. Slip the next strip through the first loop, bend it into a loop, and staple it closed. Continue adding loops to the chain until you have used the remaining strips. If you want several shorter chains, stop every so often to check your length.

LEVEL:
Easy

WHEN TO START:
1 week before the wedding

YIELD:
One 100-ft/30.5-m chain

MATERIALS
• 1 package of 100 sentence strips

TOOLS
• Stapler
• Staples

MAKING IT YOURS

Project No. 23

LEVEL:
Easy

WHEN TO START:
2 weeks before the wedding

YIELD:
50 fans

MATERIALS
- Fifty 7½-by-7½-in/19-by-19-cm blank paddle fans with wood handles
- Fifty 8½-by-11-in/21.5-by-28-cm sheets graph paper

TOOLS
- Butcher paper
- Rubber gloves
- 1 can spray adhesive
- Craft knife

SCHOOL-PAPER HAND FAN

Individual fans are terrific to have on hand for guests in the heat of the summer. You can find many shapes and sizes of fans to suit your event and have fun customizing them to suit your decor. If you like, customize your fans with words and names by printing the papers on your home printer before adhering them to the fans.

HOW TO

1. **Set up your work area.** Choose a work surface in a well-ventilated area, and cover the surface with butcher paper.

2. **Cover the fans with paper.** Wearing rubber gloves, apply a light, even coat of spray adhesive to the side of the fan without the handle. Let the glue set up for a few seconds. Smoothly lay a sheet of graph paper on the glue. Set aside to dry for about 5 minutes. Repeat to glue sheets of paper to the remaining fans.

3. **Trim the fans.** Turn each fan papered-side down and use the craft knife to trim away the excess paper, following the contour of the fan.

STYLING IDEAS

In lieu of a giant wedding cake, you could opt for a sweets buffet but still have a small cutting cake. Flank the cake with a variety of candies and treats displayed in large glass apothecary jars, on platters, and in footed bowls. A menu—drawn on a chalkboard or presented on paper with cute graphics—will help guests navigate the contents. You can supply glassine bags and ribbon ties so guests can take away their favorite.

INDUSTRIAL REVIVAL

INDUSTRIAL REVIVAL

RARELY DOES A BRIDE SAY that she wants a steampunk wedding. When Pamela approached me with her concept, I had to do a little research. Steampunk, it turns out, is a style that was inspired by the Victorian era—with a futuristic twist. Urban Dictionary describes steampunk as "what the past would look like if the future had happened sooner." Given my design theory that "everything old is new again," I was confident that I could combine a Victorian industrial atmosphere with the soft, romantic wedding details that Pamela had in mind.

She and her fiancé, Shane, had already secured one of my favorite local spots for the wedding—the Roundhouse Railroad Museum, the largest and most complete antebellum railroad repair facility still in existence, complete with historic train cars and the machinery that was necessary to keep the cars running smoothly. A historic museum can provide a great stage for a vintage-style wedding if the look matches your vision. In this case, the Victorian atmosphere was built-in, and the venue provided a sense of history and drama that intrigued everyone.

Pamela and I determined that muted grays, beige, black, and off-white, with metallic accents of silver, gold, bronze, and iron, would fit the location and the event. The scene was dotted with shades of purple, and the only other color was a touch of teal in the sash of Pamela's dress. These days, you can often select a nontraditional color scheme, so a muted range is not an unusual choice for a wedding. For this wedding, the color scheme was married to the machinery in this amazing venue, giving the wedding a sense of history and place.

Most of the visual drama would be reserved for the reception, but the bride and groom—an army major who was deployed during most of the planning—also wanted the ceremony to have an industrial steampunk style. Antique wooden folding chairs salvaged from an old country fairground filled the museum's tinder frame shop. Hand fans inscribed with the couple's names, the wedding date, and the location were placed on each chair seat. A giant pocket watch, hung from a bolt in the rustic brick wall, marked the time the ceremony would begin. The couple was married in front of a miniature replica of a steam engine, rather than near the real-life steam engine in the same room. If you choose a museum for your ceremony, having an under-stated backdrop ensures that you and not the museum displays will be the center of attention.

After the ceremony, guests enjoyed cocktails in the nearby walled garden, while the bride and groom sneaked away for a moment alone. Just before sunset, everyone went into the museum's machine shop for dinner and dancing. The rustic interior was filled with huge wheels, drills, and other antique machinery. The sign-in table was decorated with an antique store display stacked high with old papers and antique pens. Guests wrote messages to the couple, then slid them beneath a paperweight in an antique velvet box. From the table, guests picked up escort cards so they could easily move to their seats after writing their messages.

We placed more vintage folding chairs around long wooden tables along the one wall of the brick structure. The cake, set on the only skirted, round table, was the focal point. In lieu of linens, we used a single runner on each dining table. The runners were made from player piano music rolls, the type pierced with holes. The rustic wood of the tables showed through the holes, creating an interesting pattern the length of the table. Against this decorative backdrop were flower-filled ceramic medicine bottles adorned with replica labels. Candles in tall jars provided romantic tabletop lighting. Adding to the antique look, we scattered tarnished antique silver trays (if you don't like to clean silver, this is the style for you!), chemistry stands, wire domes, machine parts, and tiny decoupage glass trays with clock face engravings along the length of the tables. The layered effect felt like a collection—decorative and purposeful at the same time.

> **TIP**
>
> *Ask a friend or family member to handle all the gifts, cards, and envelopes you receive at your wedding. That person can keep everything until you are home from your honeymoon. You will have plenty of time to unwrap the gifts and read the well wishes from your guests when you return.*

The bride and groom's table was at one end of the guests' dining tables so they could sit side by side and see everyone. A large industrial band saw on the site framed their seating area, and vintage high-back chairs with pale upholstery marked their places at the table. The wedding table centerpiece fit their steampunk style: a composition of antique silver, old store counter bells, and flowers intertwined with candles and various accouterments.

The photographers occasionally snuck the couple away for photos. You can take advantage of the fantastic scenery at your site by asking your photographer to look for areas that will make memorable images. You can enhance the expression of your theme in the photos by having a few props on hand. In this case, the bride had a Victorian parasol, and the groom had old goggles, a top hat, and an antique pocket watch. Don't be afraid to move your furnishings around to create interesting arrangements. We placed one of the upholstered chairs from the head table on the railroad tracks near an old sycamore tree on the museum grounds. The beautiful composition resulted in a photo that embodied the day.

TIP *You don't have to reserve a separate set of clothes for the getaway at the end of the evening. If you anticipate a long night and that big beautiful ball gown might prove to be cumbersome on the dance floor, a change of apparel might be in order. Midway through the evening, you can sneak away and slip into a shorter, more comfy dress and shoes and still dance the night away in style.*

ANTIQUE MEDICINE JARS

For this wedding, vintage labels from an antique store were duplicated on a copy machine to provide extras. You can play with the scale on the copy machine to make labels that fit the bottles you find.

HOW TO

1. **Cut the tape.** Cut two strips of tape to match the height of a label.

2. **Attach the label.** Apply the strips of tape to opposite ends of the back of the label. Smoothly press the taped side of the label onto a bottle. Repeat the steps for the remaining labels and bottles.

MAKING IT YOURS
Project No. **24**

LEVEL:
Easy

WHEN TO START:
3 weeks before the wedding

YIELD:
50 bottles

MATERIALS
- 50 vintage or reproduction medicine bottle labels*
- 50 vintage medicine bottles

TOOLS
- Scissors
- Double-sided tape

* If you have trouble finding labels or designing your own, look for websites that allow you to download templates.

MAKING IT YOURS

Project No. 25

LEVEL:
Easy

WHEN TO START:
Day before or day of the wedding

YIELD:
1 snack suitcase

MATERIALS
- Snacks
- Celebratory beverage
- 2 glass jars with lids
- 2 brown paper lunch bags
- 2 waxed paper bags
- 1 vintage suitcase
- 2 sets of flatware
- 2 cups
- 2 cloth napkins

TO-GO SNACK SUITCASE

Couples rarely get a bite to eat at their own reception. Caterers often provide a sampling from the items served during the reception, but it is nice to have a backup. You can place the suitcase in your getaway car or have it delivered to your hotel.

HOW TO

1. **Gather the food.** Choose snacks that will keep well at room temperature, such as crackers and pretzels, slices of cured dried salami, breadsticks, fruit, nuts, cookies, and biscotti. Select a beverage that will be good at room temperature, perhaps flavored sparkling water.
2. **Pack the suitcase.** Fill the glass jars and paper bags with the snacks. Place them in the suitcase and nestle in the beverage along with the flatware, cups, and napkins.

Prop warehouses and antique shops are great places to find pretty lighting, antique tables, beautiful upholstery, unusual tables, and the like. For instance, if you want large columns or an unusual altar for your ceremony, you could contact a warehouse that stocks architectural salvage pieces. Or if you want to have your portraits taken on an antique French settee, talk with a local antique dealer about rentals. Keep in mind that shipping or pickup and delivery will have to be arranged. Some rental companies have special agreements with prop warehouses and shops so don't be shy.

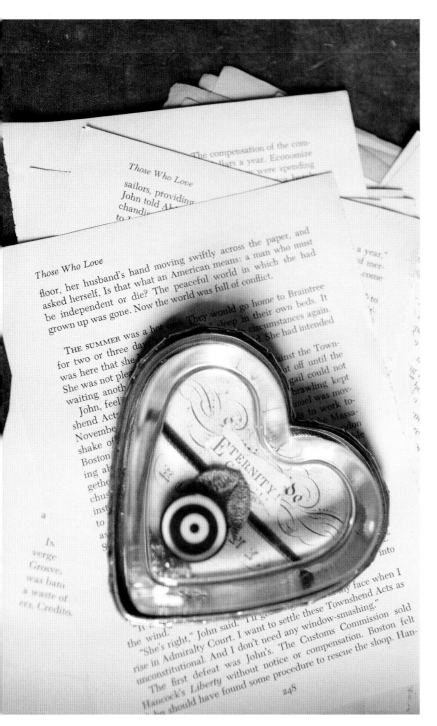

STYLING IDEAS

Traditional guest books are fine to put out at your reception, but why not use something more unusual and memorable? You can find old journals, ledgers, and receipt books and antique leather books. Guests can write on the blank pages of the journals and ledgers or directly on pages of antique books. File them away in clever boxes or antique file folder displays after the wedding and open them on your first anniversary. Remember to include attractive writing utensils that fit the look of your wedding.

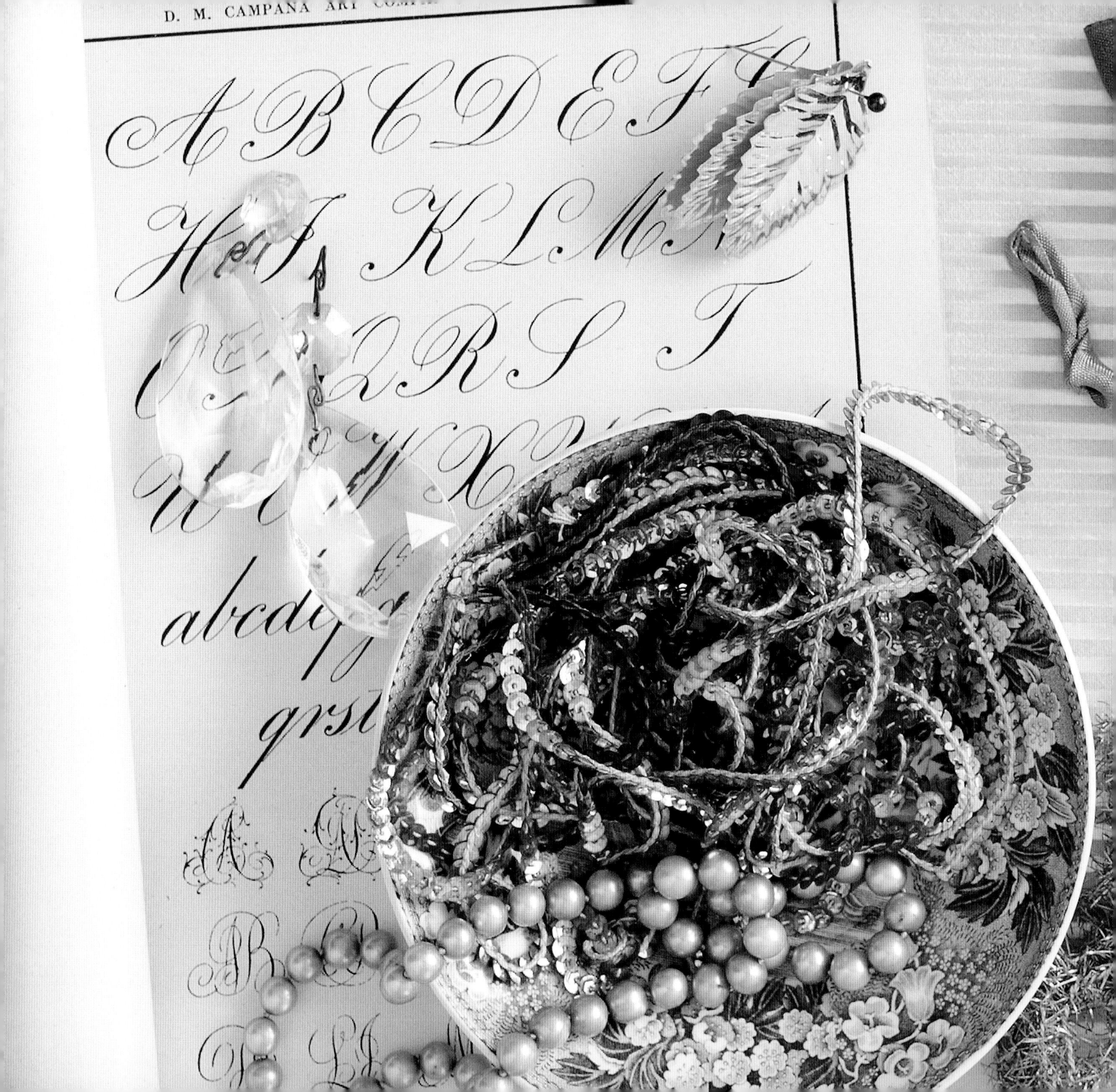
D. M. CAMPANA ART

Vintage Glam

Chapter
No. 12

Vintage Glam

MANY BRIDES ENVISION a memorable day with traditional sparkle—lush flowers, fancy food, ballroom chairs, and, yes, even crystal chandeliers. Kara dreamed of a glamorous vintage-style wedding. She and Steven did their research and chose an ideal location—a sweet little chapel on the grounds of the Bethesda Home for Boys, an eighteenth-century orphanage on five hundred acres of beautiful low country land on the banks of the Moon River. The setting was picture-perfect for the ceremony, but they had no luck finding a spot nearby for the reception. Knowing Kara's love of antiques, color, and texture, I immediately thought of the Pink House, a historic restaurant dating from the 1700s in downtown historic Savannah.

Couples often overlook restaurant venues for their reception, admittedly for good reasons: the site is sometimes hard to customize, the room may not be large enough or private enough, or the location may be too expensive. Finding the right restaurant may take some shopping around, but if you live in an area that has great restaurants with ballrooms, the search is worth the time and effort.

The ballroom of the Pink House would be a grand venue for a formal affair, so I took Kara to see it. She immediately liked the details: coastal scenes in shades of gold, silver, and gray on Zuber wallpaper, gold leaf mirrors, velvet drapes, ornate crystal chandeliers, and striking architectural moldings. We stayed for lunch and sampled a few dishes that could be nice additions to her reception menu. The only dilemma was the date. Kara

wanted to be married on New Year's Eve, a holiday when many venues and vendors charge more for gatherings. The catering tab would have doubled if she had stuck to this date, but I convinced her to marry on New Year's Day instead. She agreed it would be a wonderful way to start the new year.

The beauty of a restaurant reception is that you don't have to import the basics—restaurants come equipped with tables, chairs, lighting, dishes, glasses, and flatware. Plus, they offer trained servers and a well-stocked bar. Having these details covered allows you to concentrate on the fun, decorative stuff. We enhanced the glamour of the ballroom by dressing up the tables with opulent flower arrangements in shades of purple and dark pinks, luxurious gray table covers, and sparkly purple, silver, and gold mercury glass flower vessels and candleholders.

We also booked a small adjacent room with a decidedly masculine appeal. The comfortable leather club chairs, large fireplace, and french doors opening onto a terrace were so appealing that the room became a welcome spot for those wanting to escape the loud music or sit for a moment by the fire.

With all the reception details in place, we focused our attention on the ceremony. Bethesda's Whitfield Chapel, with its antique pine pews and herringbone-patterned brick floor, has a lot of character on its own. It is a small chapel—built in 1925 to serve the students and barely large enough to seat a hundred people—and is beautiful in its architectural simplicity. The large Palladian

windows cast enough light inside so that the space could be lit with soft candlelight alone. In each windowsill, we placed arrangements of greenery atop antique silver trays. The bride's aunt made magnolia leaf wreaths for the chapel's large paneled doors. This is a very Southern touch, as magnolia leaves are the holiday equivalent of pine boughs and holly. As guests arrived, they were given programs I had bound on my sewing machine—an effective and attractive way to make your own programs. A solitary candle stood at the front of the chapel as a memorial to the groom's mother.

In keeping with the elegance of the occasion, a string ensemble entertained before the ceremony and provided the wedding music. Kara looked like a Hollywood starlet straight out of the 1940s in her one-shoulder gown with vintage rhinestone appliqués, and her long hair pinned up under a vintage-inspired cage veil.

The bridal party and guests left the chapel and headed to the Pink House, where the glamorous ballroom promised a sparkling, fun-filled reception party. When guests arrived, they saw a sign painted on an antique mirror that read "Wisdom and Wishes for the Mr. and Mrs.," prompting them to write to Kara or Steven or to both using the cards and pens provided. (This was a little cheeky, but guests could give different advice depending on the recipient.) The sign-in table held three ballot boxes, each

TIP

Before you decide to have your wedding on or around a holiday, you want to consider a few things. Travel for both you and your guests might be difficult or expensive. Hotels' rates could be higher, and venues may include a surcharge for staying open and staffed on holidays. On the flip side, holiday weddings can be very beautiful and memorable.

identifying the recipient of the note. Some guests wrote notes for all three boxes, some to one or the other. At the end of the night, I packaged all the notes so that I could present them to the couple a few weeks later. I'm sure they had many laughs reading them to each other—that is, if they decided to share.

Hors d'oeuvres and cocktails were passed around the crowded restaurant as music pulsed throughout the night. Kara wanted to encourage mingling but didn't want to skimp on food. She asked the restaurant to do a progressive service with waiters circulating with trays of small portions. Three courses—a typical meal—were served, but in appetizer portions, which allowed guests to sit, stand, talk, dance, or mingle as they wished. The first round of trays contained salads and appetizers, followed by heartier dishes like beef tenderloin crostini and crab cakes, and so on, until the last round of desserts was passed.

Kara and Steven are avid swing dancers, and an evening of merriment, food, and dancing was enjoyed by all. Candlelight and fragrant flowers filled the room, fireplaces burned merrily, and the chandeliers sparkled and spread their light throughout. It was a beautiful way to ring in the New Year and their new life together.

TIP

At your reception, you may want to set aside a quiet space for guests who prefer conversation to the sound of a band or DJ. You and your groom may also appreciate taking a moment away from the crowds.

The wedding of

Kara Elizabeth Powers

and

Steven Matthew Olmsted

January 1, 2011
Savannah, Georgia

SEWN PROGRAMS

Programs are a handy way to share with your guests the schedule of the ceremony, information about the bridal party, music selections, and memorials, but they don't need to be fussy or expensive. Making self-sewn programs can save a bundle and allow you to personalize the look for your wedding. These programs are four pages, but you can include up to eight.

HOW TO

1. **Print the programs.** Using a word processing program, choose an attractive font and design and lay out your program. Create a cover with your names. For the three pages inside, consider including text from the ceremony, a poem, and/or a schedule of the event. When arranging the content, allow a ¼-in/6-mm margin on the left side of each page to accommodate the stitched binding. Print the pages onto the cardstock. Collate the pages into fifty programs.

2. **Stitch the programs.** Set your sewing machine for a straight stitch. Use one hand to hold the pages of each program and the other hand to guide them under the presser foot. Sew the pages together, leaving a ⅛-in/3-mm seam allowance. Use the scissors to trim the thread, leaving a ½-in/12-mm fringe to finish.

MAKING IT YOURS
Project No. 26

LEVEL:
Moderate

WHEN TO START:
1 week before the wedding

YIELD:
50 four-page programs

MATERIALS
• Two hundred 5½-by-8½-in/
  14-by-21.5-cm sheets card stock
• Thread

TOOLS
• Word processing program
• Laser or inkjet printer
• Sewing machine with a needle
  for heavyweight fabrics
• Scissors

LEVEL:
Moderate

WHEN TO START:
4 weeks before the wedding

YIELD:
3 ballot boxes

MATERIALS
• 3 wooden boxes with lids
• Cards

TOOLS
• Tape measure
• Pencil
• Dremel rotary tool with ¼-in/
  6-mm router bit
• 120-grit sandpaper
• Stain marker
• 3 decorative rubber stamps
• Ink pad

BALLOT BOX SIGN-IN

Instead of using the traditional sign-in book, you can come up with creative ways for guests to leave you a message. Making the experience interesting for guests will inspire them to participate. Arrange the boxes in a line on the sign-in table. Place a stack of fifty 4-by-6-in/10-by-15-cm cards in front of each box. Set pens out for the guests. Use place cards and holders to designate one box for the bride, one for the groom, and one for both.

HOW TO

1. **Cut openings in the boxes.** Using the tape measure and pencil, mark the center of each box lid. With that mark as your reference, measure and draw a 4¼-in-/10.5-cm-long line, centered across each lid. Use the Dremel tool to rout that line and create an opening for sliding the cards into the box. The opening should measure ¼ in/6 mm wide. Lightly sand the edges of the opening on each box lid. If the boxes are dark wood, finish the opening by running the stain marker along the cut surface.

2. **Decorate the cards.** Use the rubber stamps and ink pad to embellish the blank cards. Alternate stamp designs and positions to create a random assortment to finish.

STYLING IDEAS

Antique frames, with or without mirrors, can add a lot of character to a venue. In the entryway of this wedding, a Victorian framed mirror was used as a sign and embellished with a silk prize ribbon in the palette of the wedding. You could use mirrors for signage, table assignments, or a menu, or simply hang them in your reception area to reflect light. Collect many frames and attach them to one another to create a unique backdrop for your nuptials. Consider painting them all one color to reinforce your palette.

Wisdom and wishes for the Mr. and Mrs.

TIP

Honoring relatives who have passed away comes up often when planning a wedding. You can pay tribute to loved ones and have them present on your special day by asking the officiant to mention them, or placing photos of them at your reception, or saying something about them in your program. As a symbolic statement, you can put a solitary posy in a vase in an honored spot at your ceremony location.

Resources

REVIVING GATSBY

Location:
R. J. Reynolds Mansion, Sapelo Island, GA

Photography:
Something Pretty
www.andsomethingpretty.com

Susan Dean Photography
www.susandeanphoto.com

Jade + Matthew Take Pictures
www.jadeandmatthew.com

Wedding Dress:
Bridal Couture by Ruby V

Invitations:
Royal Steamline
www.royalsteamline.com

Cake topper:
The Small Object
www.thesmallobject.com

Weekend agenda, Western Union
message, and postcards:
Hein van der Heijden
www.deshein.com

Boxes:
The Container Store
www.containerstore.com

Wooden hanger:
eBay
www.ebay.com

Ribbon and millinery leaves:
Tinsel Trading Company
www.tinseltrading.com

TWO-RING CIRCUS

Location:
Meldrim Woods Plantation, Brooklet, GA

Photography:
Orange Slice Weddings
www.orangesliceweddings.com

Jade + Matthew Take Pictures
www.jadeandmatthew.com

Wedding dress:
Chelsea Rose Bridal
www.chelsea-rose.net

Bride's headpiece:
Haylie Waring
www.hayliebird.blogspot.com

Invitations:
Meagan Bennett
www.meggsbenedict.tumblr.com

Cake topper:
Jennifer Murphy
www.jmurphybears.com

Cake topper banner:
Katie Runnels
www.theconstantgatherer.com

Balloons:
Shop Sweet Lulu
www.shopsweetlulu.com

Straw hand fans:
Asian Ideas
www.asianideas.com

Tissue paper buntings:
Oriental Trading
www.orientaltrading.com

UP IN THE CLOUDS

Location:
Jekyll Island Club, Jekyll Island, GA

Photography:
Blue Door Photography
www.blue-doorphotography.com

Jade + Matthew Take Pictures
www.jadeandmatthew.com

Wedding dress:
Mitchell Hall
(314) 412-5055

Invitations and save-the-dates:
Belle & Union Co.
www.belleandunion.com

Paper parasols and paper lanterns:
Luna Bazaar
www.lunabazaar.com

Vintage bottles and maps:
eBay
www.ebay.com

Etsy
www.etsy.com

Muslin bags:
Uline
www.uline.com

Rubber stamps:
A1Stamps
www.a1stamps.com

FALL COLOR

Location:
Old Fort Jackson, Savannah, GA

Photography:
Julia Robbs for Our Labor of Love
www.ourlaboroflove.com

Wedding dress:
The Clothing Warehouse
www.theclothingwarehouse.com

Bride's Headpiece:
Twigs and Honey
www.twigsandhoney.com

Cake topper:
Monica Lynch
www.etsy.com/shop/LettieBriggs

Bouquet, programs, napkin ties, and illustrations:
Jessica Duthu
www.jessicaduthu.com

Wool fibers, felting needles, and millinery leaves:
Tinsel Trading Company
www.tinseltrading.com

Michaels
www.michaels.com

Hobby Lobby
www.hobbylobby.com

Lanterns:
Ikea
www.ikea.com

AIRSTREAM ELOPEMENT

Location:
Forsyth Park, Savannah, GA

Photography:
Jade + Matthew Take Pictures
www.jadeandmatthew.com

Wedding dress:
Designs by Malyse
www.designsbymalyse.com

Balloons:
Shop Sweet Lulu
www.shopsweetlulu.com

Ribbon:
Tinsel Trading Company
www.tinseltrading.com

Picnic goods:
Shop Sweet Lulu
www.shopsweetlulu.com

Reliable Paper
www.reliablepaper.com

Alphabet rubber stamps:
Paper Source
www.papersource.com

Michaels
www.michaels.com

Hobby Lobby
www.hobbylobby.com

OLD FORT

Location:
Old Fort Jackson, Savannah, GA

Photography:
Juliet Elizabeth Photography
www.julietelizabeth.com

Jade + Matthew Take Pictures
www.jadeandmatthew.com

Wedding dress:
Amy Kuschel
www.amykuschel.com

Number hooks:
Two's Company
www.twoscompany.com

Paper fans:
BHLDN
www.bhldn.com

Glass test tubes:
Lake Charles Manufacturing
www.lcmlab.com

eBay
www.ebay.com

FLEA MARKET CHARM

Location:
Magnolia Hall Plantation,
Charleston, SC

Photography:
Juliet Elizabeth Photography
www.julietelizabeth.com

Jade + Matthew Take Pictures
www.jadeandmatthew.com

Wedding dress:
Paloma Blanca
www.palomablanca.com

Paper bells, antique doilies, antique jars, vintage sheet music, and antique china:
eBay
www.ebay.com

Etsy
www.etsy.com

Paperweight kits:
Two's Company
www.twoscompany.com

FARMHOUSE FETE

Location:
Beaver Dam, Davidson, NC

Photography:
Blue Door Photography
www.blue-doorphotography.com

Jade + Matthew Take Pictures
www.jadeandmatthew.com

Wedding dress:
J. Crew
www.jcrew.com

Cake topper, boutonnieres, felt letters, and save-the-dates:
Holly Sexton
www.hollysexton.com

Invitations, programs and wine labels:
The Lettered Lily
www.theletteredlily.com

Ribbon:
Tinsel Trading Company
www.tinseltrading.com

Clear acrylic bowls and baskets:
Party City
www.partycity.com

Patterned wax paper:
Etsy
www.etsy.com

DaWanda
en.dawanda.com

LOVELY DAY

Location:
Private residence, Savannah, GA

Photography:
Jade + Matthew Take Pictures
www.jadeandmatthew.com

Wedding dress:
The Limited
www.thelimited.com/bridal

Bride's headpiece, ring hoop, handkerchiefs, and men's accessories:
French Knot
www.frenchknotweddings.com

Aisle markers, boutonnieres, and bunting:
Andrea Gray Harper
www.grayharper.com

Invitations, table top games, signs, and tags:
Belle & Union Co
www.belleandunion.com

Crepe paper folds:
Crepe Paper Store
www.crepepaperstore.com

SCHOOLHOUSE ROCK

Location:
Old Sheldon Ruins, Beaufort, SC
(ceremony)

The Morris Center, Savannah, GA
(reception)

Photography:
Jade + Matthew Take Pictures
www.jadeandmatthew.com

Wedding dress:
Maggie Sottero
www.maggiesottero.com

**Invitations, save-the-dates, and
thank-you cards:**
Belle & Union Co
www.belleandunion.com

Cake topper:
The Small Object
www.thesmallobject.com

Glass apothecary jars:
Save-on-Crafts
www.save-on-crafts.com

Candy:
Candy Warehouse
www.candywarehouse.com

Manila sentence strips:
Staples
www.staples.com

Blank paddle fans:
Kiefer Auction Supply
www.kieferauctionsupply.com

INDUSTRIAL REVIVAL

Location:
Roundhouse Railroad Museum,
Savannah, GA

Photography:
Jade + Matthew Take Pictures
www.jadeandmatthew.com

Wedding dress:
White dress, vintage

Bride's gray dress
April Johnston
www.themangledcourtesan.com

Clock face plates:
Two's Company
www.twoscompany.com

**Antique pharmacy labels, medicine
bottles, vintage luggage, and antique silver:**
eBay
www.ebay.com

Etsy
www.etsy.com

VINTAGE GLAM

Location:
Whitefield Chapel, Bethesda Home for Boys,
Savannah, GA (ceremony)

The Olde Pink House, Savannah, GA
(reception)

Photography:
Millie Holloman Photography
www.millieholloman.com

Wedding dress:
Platinum Priscilla of Boston
www.pricillaofboston.com

Bride's headpiece:
Maria Elena
www.mariaelenaheadpieces.com

Wooden boxes:
Michaels
www.michaels.com

Rubber stamps:
Paper Source
www.papersource.com

Michaels
www.michaels.com

Hobby Lobby
www.hobbylobby.com

The photographs in this book are copyright © of the following companies.

Blue Door Photography: pages 44, 46–51, 56–57, 100, 122, 124–130, 133–135

Jade + Matthew Take Pictures: pages 10–11, 21–22, 26–27, 37, 42–43, 53, 58–59, 76–78, 80–82, 85–89, 96, 99, 104–105, 111, 114, 118, 120–121, 133, 136–138, 140–144, 147–149, 150–152, 154–160, 163–168, 170–176, 179–183

Juliet Elizabeth Photography: pages 90, 92–95, 102–103, 106, 108–113, 117–119

Millie Holloman Photography: pages 184, 186–190, 193–195

Orange Slice Photography: pages 28, 30–35, 39–42

Our Labor of Love: pages 60, 62–68, 71–72, 74–75

Something Pretty Photography: pages 5, 12, 14–18, 24

Susan Dean Photography: pages 14–18, 21, 24, 25

GENERAL RESOURCES AND INSPIRATION

EYE CANDY

100 Layer Cake
www.100layercake.com

Anthology Magazine
www.anthologymag.com

Brides Café
www.bridescafe.com

Glamour and Grace Blog
www.glamourandgraceblog.com

Mag Rouge
www.magrouge.com

Once Wed
www.oncewed.com

Postcards and Pretties
www.postcardsandpretties.blogspot.com

Ritzy Bee
www.ritzybee.typepad.com

Rue Magazine
www.ruemag.com

Ruffled Blog
www.ruffledblog.com

Snippet and Ink
www.snippetandink.com

Southern Weddings
www.iloveswmag.com

Style Me Pretty
www.stylemepretty.com

The Bride's Guide
www.thebridesguide.marthastewart
weddings.com

Utterly Engaged
www.utterlyengaged.com

PAPER EYE CANDY (MAGAZINES)

Brides

DIY Weddings Magazine

Get Married

Grace Ormond

Inside Weddings

Martha Stewart Weddings

Real Simple Weddings

Southern Weddings

Southern Living Weddings

The Knot Magazine

Town and Country Weddings

Weddings Unveiled

SWEETS & FANCIFUL PACKAGING

Acme Party Box
www.acmepartybox.com

Bake it Pretty
www.bakeitpretty.com

Blair Candy
www.blaircandy.com

Bulk Party Supplies
www.bulkpartysupplies.com

A Candy Store
www.acandystore.com

Candy Warehouse
www.candywarehouse.com

Hope and Greenwood
www.hopeandgreenwood.co.uk

Lette Macarons
www.lettemacarons.com

Reliable Paper
www.reliablepaper.com

Shop Sweet Lulu
www.shopsweetlulu.com

The Container Store
www.containerstore.com

VINTAGE AND VINTAGE INSPIRED BITS, BAUBLES, FROCKS & MISCELLANEOUS WEDDING-ISH GOODS

1st Dibs
www.1stdibs.com

ABC Carpet and Home
www.abchome.com

Anthropologie
www.anthropologie.com

Ban.do
www.shopbando.com

Bella Umbrella
www.bellaumbrella.com

BHLDN
www.bhldn.com

eBay
www.ebay.com

Etsy
www.etsy.com

Fishs Eddy
www.fishseddy.com

Hyman Handler
www.hymanhendler.com

Modcloth
www.modcloth.com

Midori Ribbon
www.midoriribbon.com

Mokuba
www.mokubany.com

Paper Valise
www.papervalise.com

Poppytalk Handmade
www.poppytalkhandmade.com

Ruche
www.shopruche.com

Three Potato Four
www.threepotatofourshop.com

Tinsel Trading Company
www.tinseltrading.com

Tulle
www.tulle4us.com

V.V. Rouleaux
www.vvrouleaux.com

THE BASICS

BHS
www.bhs.co.uk

Crate and Barrel
www.crateandbarrel.com

Habitat
www.habitat.co.uk

Ikea
www.ikea.com

John Lewis
www.johnlewis.com

Muji
www.muji.com

Oriental Trading
www.orientaltrading.com

MATERIALS, TOOLS, SUPPLIES

Asian Ideas
www.asianideas.com

Etsy
www.etsy.com

Fabric Direct
www.fabricdirect.com

Happy Tape
www.happytape.bigcartel.com

Hobby Lobby
www.hobbylobby.com

Luna Bazaar
www.lunabazaar.com

Michaels
www.michaels.com

Save on Crafts
www.save-on-crafts.com

Spoon Flower
www.spoonflower.com

ANTIQUE FAIRS, FLEA MARKETS & ESTATE SALES

United States

Alameda Point Antique Fair
www.antiquesbythebay.net

Brimfield Antique Show
www.brimfieldshow.com

Estate & Garage Sales
www.craigslist.com

Hells Kitchen Flea Market
www.hellskitchenfleamarket.com

Raleigh Flea Market
www.raleighfleamarket.net

Renninger's Mount Dora
www.renningers.com

Rose Bowl
www.rgcshows.com

Round Top Antique Show
www.roundtoptexasantiques.com

Scott Antique Market
www.scottantiquemarket.com

Springfield Antique Show
www.springfieldantiqueshow.com

Great Britain

Camden Passage
www.camdenpassageislington.co.uk

Newark International Antique &
Collectors Fair
www.iacf.co.uk

Portobello Road
www.portobellomarket.org

Acknowledgments

I thank everyone who helped in the making of this book for your support, inspiration, and devotion, as well as the beautiful brides and handsome grooms who agreed to be featured, the photographers who contributed, and the many people who have inspired me to follow my instincts over the years.

Thanks to my husband, Paul, and my son, William, for their love and support, even when the dining room table was covered with craft supplies, paper pom-poms filled the hallway, and countless buckets of flowers appeared, disappeared, and reappeared. To my mother for always saying, "we can make that," because I think that stuck with me, and now I really believe it is possible to make just about anything; and to my late father for giving me such a strong work ethic. To my Aunt Rita for showing me that people can make a living in creative fields—who knew? To David Anger for opening that first door into the editorial world. To Francis Bailey for making it clear that event design was a career tailor-made for me. To my friend and agent Janice Shay for never giving up on me, even when I couldn't imagine why someone would let me write a book. To my champion team of editors at Chronicle Books: Kate Woodrow, Laura Lee Mattingly, and Micaela Heekin for providing their expertise along the way. To designer Kristen Hewitt for making it all come together beautifully. To Brookelynn Morris, the best technical writer any girl could ever wish for. To Meg Sutton, for more favors, brainstorming sessions, and all around counsel than I can count. To Paula Danyluk, sounding board and cheerleader. To Peggy Polk and Sylvia Fraser, the first people to share the glorious world of antique fairs, auctions, and estate sales—my pocketbook has never been the same but my house sure does look nice. To my dear family and friends for always believing and supporting my crazy endeavors. It looks like it's finally paying off.

Special recognition to all of the amazing couples featured:
Shane and Michelle
Adam and Halligan
Seth and Elizabeth
Terry and Jessica
Adam and Monica
Morgan and Emily
Kirk and Ashley
Daniel and Holly
Josh and Amy
Charles and Jazmin
Shane and Pamela
Steven and Kara

I also want to recognize the many artists, designers, woodworkers, illustrators, photographers, family members and friends who generously contributed their talents, advice, time, services, props, and stellar locations: Blue Door Photography, Jade + Matthew Take Pictures, Juliet Elizabeth Photography, Our Labor of Love, Something Pretty Photography, Susan Dean Photography, Orange Slice Photography, Millie Holloman Photography, Christine Hall Photography, Belle & Union Co., Halligan and Adam Smith, Jennifer Kopf, Erin Fountain, Sarah Girard, James Kirton, Lovelane Designs, Bradford Woodworking, Back in the Day Bakery, Vintage Catiques and Paul Garguilo Fine Woodworking. A special thank you to *Country Living* magazine for the use of photography for Two Ring Circus.

Index

Index